CHAPLIN

Denis Gifford

Doubleday & Co. Inc.
Garden City, New York, 1974

Who is Mr Chaplin?   *Mahatma Ghandi*

He has revived one of the great arts of
the ancient world.   *Winston Churchill*

He is the pantomimist sublime.   *Sarah Bernhardt*

He is the one genius created by the
cinema.   *George Bernard Shaw*

He is an inspired tragedian.   *Robert E. Sherwood*

He is a wonderful musician.   *Ivor Novello*

He is a document which already
qualifies as an historical event.   *Berthold Brecht*

He is your good child who puts out
his tongue as he works.   *Jean Cocteau*

He has made the world laugh.   *Minnie Maddern Fiske*

He does not give you the impression of a
happy man.   *W. Somerset Maugham*

He is an alien guilty of a degree of
moral turpitude which disqualifies him
from citizenship.   *Westbrook Pegler*

He is a goddam ballet dancer.   *W. C. Fields*

He never throws pies at home.   *Sydney Earle Chaplin*

I am a citizen of the world.   *Charles Spencer Chaplin*

Picture Acknowledgements

Most of the illustrations are from the author's
own collection. Our thanks to the following for
help with additional material – Davidson-Dalling
Associates, the British Film Institute and the
Cinema Bookshop.

1
His
Trysting Place
(1972)

THE KEYSTONE FILM CO.

Cinema has two symbols, two little figures that are recognized around the world wherever films are known and shown. One is ten inches tall, golden, and is the highest award Hollywood has to bestow. They call him Oscar. The other is five-foot-six inches tall, wears a bowler hat and a little moustache, carries a cane, has flat feet, and is the funniest man who has ever lived. He answers to the name of Charlie.

Charlie and Oscar met face to face for the first time on the night of 11 April 1972. It was a night to remember for them both. Oscar was 44 years old, Charlie 82. The President of the Academy of Motion Picture Arts and Sciences, screenwriter Daniel Taradash, stepped to the microphone and announced that this year, in addition to the regular Academy Awards, a special presentation of an Honorary Oscar was about to be made. It would go to 'an actor, a writer, a director, a producer, and a composer'. And out came one man. Silver-haired, small, shaking; red-faced, wet-eyed, waving. Charles Chaplin . . . Charlie Chaplin . . . Charlie.

Charles Spencer Chaplin had come a long way to a attend the ceremony at the Los Angeles Music Center that night. Not just from his home in distant Switzerland, but from the more distant corners of Victorian London. He had come from the Cockney gutters of the Elephant and Castle, the oppressive orphanages of Hanwell, the grim workhouses of Lambeth. He had come from the music halls of the East End, and the Folies of Paris; from the vaudevilles of the East Side and the burlesques of the Midwest. He had come from the suburban studios of primitive Hollywood and the creation of one of the mightiest combines in movies. He had come through marriages and divorces, insults and accusations, law-suits and scandals, and a twenty-year exile. And on the way he had made more people laugh than any other man in the history of the world.

And so, on a night when bright new stars like Gene Hackman and smart new movies like *The French Connection* were winning the Oscars, it was touching to see the hard heart of Hollywood moved by a memory; a surprise to find that the climax to the night could be an award for a man who had not made a film for fifteen years. It brought the city's élite to their feet to cheer and cheer again the little fellow who shuffled out to take his Oscar with tears in his eyes.

Charlie could hardly speak. 'Words seem so futile,' he said, 'so feeble.' The sentiment was a summation of Chaplin's creed as a movie maker, for his finest films, the ones that make the whole world laugh, have no words. They are silent. The sound is made by the audience – the sound of laughter.

KEYSTONE

2
His
Prehistoric Past
(1889-1913)

THE KEYSTONE FILM CO.

He has the cheek and impudence
To call his mother his ma.
Since Jack Jones come into a little bit of splosh,
Why, he don't know where he are.

The deputy for Dainty and Talented Lily Harvey, Serio-comedienne, Impersonator, Dancer and laryngitie, was no Gus Elen, but he sang that comedian's latest success as if he were the king of the costers himself – and promptly came into a little bit of splosh. As hard-earned ha'pennies rained around his curly head, Charles Chaplin Junior, little Charlie Harley, stopped in mid-stanza to scoop them up, raising a laugh, and the ante, for the first of many times. The more he scrambled, the more they laughed, the more they threw. The hard-bitten army crowd in the Aldershot Canteen were treating the substitute singer to a preview of what the world had up its sleeve for him. And if some soldier had told him that he would become one of the funniest and richest men in the world, he would have believed them. A five-year-old will believe anything.

Charles Spencer Chaplin was born on 16 April 1889 in East Lane, London[1] or Fontainebleau, France,[2] according to which of his autobiographies you read. Or Bermondsey[3] or Paris,[4] according to which of his biographers you prefer. Or 287 Kennington Road[5] or Chester Street, Kennington[6] or 3 Parnell Terrace,[7] according to which friend or relation you fancy. Or was it Pownell, Pownall, or Pownhall, as Chaplin himself pronounces it? His birth certificate has never been traced. But what is incontestible is his thoroughly theatrical descent; both his parents were of the stage.

Charles Chaplin the elder had a burst of small glory on the Victorian music halls. From his earliest appearance in 1885 as a mimic of other, larger talents, through a period as a singer of Dramatic and Descriptive Ballads, the first Charles Chaplin soon climbed to the coloured covers of contemporary song hits. There was *Pals that Time Cannot Alter*, there was *Oui! Tray Bong!* and *Every-Day Life*, and there was *The Girl Was Young and Pretty* which bore the legend 'Written, composed and sung with the greatest success by Charles Chaplin, published by Howard & Co.'. Contemporaries compared him in looks with Charles Godfrey ('the two were often taken for brothers') but we would compare him with his son. The hair, the eyes, the teeth, the smile: draw a blot under the nose and there stands Charlie.

Mrs Chaplin, Hannah Hill with an Irish father and a half-gypsy mother, called herself Lily Harley for the halls. She had sung in Gilbert and Sullivan, impersonated in variety, and once, it is said, appeared on a song cover herself, in full colour, wearing a wig and gown, as a lady of law. In 1885 as a girl of eighteen, Hannah had eloped to South Africa. The man was a middle-aged Lord, she told little Charlie; actually he was a

Jewish bookmaker named Hawkes. Almost immediately her first son, Sydney junior, was born. A year later she was home and alone, caring for her baby at her father's cobbler shop off the Walworth Road, and marrying her old love, Charles Chaplin, Topical Vocalist. Three years passed before Sydney had a half-brother, and two years more before both Syd and Charlie had another. Guy Dryden arrived, then Wheeler Dryden; Charles Chaplin Senior departed.

The downward slide began. To keep her first two boys Hannah went back on the halls, but her power was gone and her voice going. She could still dance, however, and joined the Katti Lanner ballet at the Empire Theatre, Leicester Square. She took her youngest son with her every night; Syd, four years older, could look after himself. Little Charlie loved the busy, noisy, paint and bright lights world of backstage theatre, where he was fussed over by the ladies of the chorus: it was a nightly trip to heated heaven after the cold and dark of the Lambeth slums.

Nellie Richards, a music hall star of the nineties, was found in the ranks of the Elstree extras in 1931. She recalled the boy Charlie, and how she had smacked him 'where he sat down – and more than once! He was a regular little demon at times. He would stop there in the wings, singing my choruses half a line ahead of me, and so vigorously that I'm sure people in front must have heard him. The harder I frowned at him, the wider he grinned, and went right on with it. I was always threatening to spank him, so usually he ran like a hare when the last lines of my song were on my lips.'[9] Charlie's favourite songs, recalled Nellie, were *Hush Little Baby, Don't You Cry* and *I'm So Lonely, Oh So Lonely* – significant titles, indeed – 'but he had a wonderful ear for music even then, and picked up almost everything I sang'.

Charlie was a darling: his old schoolteacher, Mrs E. Turner-Dauncey, wrote 'I taught Charlie Chaplin at the Victory Place Board School in Walworth, London, when he was aged between four and five. I well remember his large eyes, his mass of dark, curly hair, and his beautiful hands. He was very sweet and so shy.'[10] Adds Nellie Richards, 'Charlie has his mother's eyes, and many of her characteristics as well'. The physical inheritance came through nature, but the intellectual inheritance was something more. Hannah's songs and stories, dances and impersonations, private performances for a little boy to brighten the nights of poverty, these were the seeds from which the world's greatest entertainer grew.

'It seems to me that my mother was the most splendid woman I ever knew. I can remember how charming and well-mannered she was. She spoke four languages fluently and had a good education. I have met a lot of people knocking around the world since; but I have never met a more thoroughly refined woman than my mother. If I have

amounted to anything, or ever do amount to anything, it will be due to her.'[11] Charles Chaplin in 1915; the first of many tributes he would pay Hannah.

But that was twenty-two years in the future: back in 1894 bookings for Lily Harley were falling, and if she had not been forced by circumstance to drag her youngest around with her, there would have been no pennies that night at the Aldershot Canteen. Her husband, now living with a lady called Louise, was on the slide, too. Charles Chaplin was going the way of so many of his entertaining ilk: he had succumbed to the Demon Drink. There was now no alternative for his abandoned family but that other great Victorian institution, the Poorhouse. In the register of the Hanwell Schools for Orphans and Destitute Children there is a famous entry.

Chaplin, Charles, aged 7, Protestant.
Admitted on the 18th June, 1896.
Left to return to his mother, 18th January, 1898.

Eighteen months of hell for a very little boy, torn from both loving mother and protective half-brother by the rule that separated siblings into Big Boys and Infants. At the end of it all Syd was sent to sea, while Charles Chaplin Senior made grudging arrangements for his only son.

John Willie Jackson, a white lead worker of Golborne near Manchester, was a widower with four children. He taught them all clog dancing and advertised for a wife. Then he had another child and taught him to clog dance, too. Adding the three dancing sons of Mrs Cawley, a local widow, J.W. chopped short the hair of his only daughter, Rosie, and billed the lot as 'The Eight Lancashire Lads'. The toe-tapping team quickly caught on, first in the North where clog dancing had its annual championships, then in the South. But there came a day when the Eight Lancashire Lads turned suddenly into seven. J.W. went forth in search of another Lad; it was cheaper than changing the posters.

Charlie Chaplin, the East End kid, had never been near Lancashire in his life. But that didn't matter to J. W. Jackson; all that mattered was that the boy could dance. He had a natural rhythm, pleasing enough to coax coins from the Cockneys as he hopped to the jangle of the street barrel organs. Charles Senior made the arrangements: half a crown a week for Hannah, board and lodging for Charlie. And so, with his formal education completed after eighteen months with the Orphans and Destitute Children, Charlie Chaplin went dancing down the showbiz road to fame and fortune.

The tour, which took Charlie far from home, had its miseries, even for a boy whose home life had not been exactly stable. But it also had its joys. Charlie shared the stage with every class of vaudeville performer, from humble jugglers like Zarmo the Tramp to all-time bill-toppers like Marie Lloyd.

His talent for mimicry, inherited from both Hannah and Charles, began to shine. He studied the stars and copied their mannerisms. J.W., ever alert for a gimmick, saw Charlie's takeoff of Bransby Williams, acclaimed delineator of Dickens characters. He bundled the boy on stage, a bald wig topping his standard Lad uniform of blouse and knickerbockers. That night, for the first time, the Death of Little Nell drew a different kind of tears. Neither Charlie nor J.W. saw the significance of this laughter, and the Added Attraction was instantly withdrawn from the act.

Charles Chaplin did well out of his small son. He shelved the responsibility of his keep and his schooling, and when he was so far down in the drink that the business had to throw him a Grand Benefit to keep him out of the Poorhouse, Charlie came and clogged for his dad with the rest of the Lancashire Lads. Half a century later the world sang Charlie Chaplin's song, *Smile while your heart is breaking*; but there was no pre-echo of the sentiment in his performance that night. To young Charlie his father had been scarce more than a shadow: a shadow with a red face whose 'breath was hot and strong with whisky'.[2]

Charlie cocks a snook

above: *Between Showers* (1914)

right: *Shanghaied* (1915)

The Hippodrome, 'London's Latest and Greatest Pleasure Resort', previewed its first pantomime on the afternoon of Wednesday, 26 December, 1900: the traditional Boxing Day début. *Cinderella* it was, played by Amy Farrell, and Buttons, the funny-sad figure who loved her and lost her, was Marceline. As the kitchen cat, Charlie Chaplin shared one scene with the famous French clown. He lapped milk from a saucer, arched his back, caused Buttons to fall, and winked one big eye at the audience. The laugh he received touched something deep in the eleven year old clog-dancer. He wanted more, and went after it. The audience gasped as the pantomime cat suddenly capered up to the rear end of the pantomime dog – and sniffed! They roared, and roared again as puss turned his head and gave them another big wink. The manager rushed into the wings to see what this new laughter was about. He saw the cat sniffing the scenery, then lifting its back leg in a very uncatlike gesture! The world's first Chaplin gag had been born.

Analyse this gag and you find the formula for an entire comedy career to come. Its basis was incongruity: the simple switch. A cat behaving like its opposite, a dog. The behaviour itself: fundamental, universal, lavatorial. The build-up: from one small joke, an elaboration on the theme, until a climax is reached and the new laughs, coming on top of old laughs not yet dead, erupt in the only possible relief, applause. The form: visual. The gag needed no words of explanation. Above all, the spontaneity: the gag was unexpected, by the audience, and almost by the creator. It flashed into Chaplin's mind in an instant of time, and was executed in that instant, before it

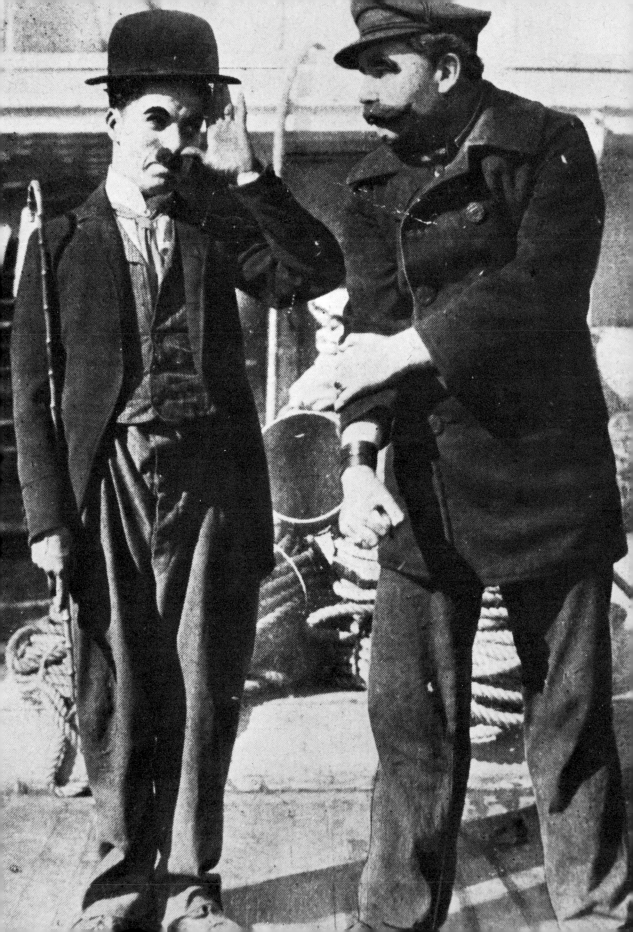

could be considered, constructed, made concrete. Spontaneity: the first word future film critics would apply to Chaplin comedy. Charlie's gag threw the manager into a fury. 'Never do that again', he cried. 'You'll have the Lord Chamberlain close down the theatre!' And so, finally, the joke discloses one more basic trait of its creator: for the first time of many Chaplin upset the censors.

The final performance of *Cinderella* took place on the night of Saturday, 13 April 1901. Three days later Charlie was twelve. Three weeks later his father was dead. *The Era* said it all:

> Our readers will hear with regret, but without surprise, of the death of poor Charles Chaplin, the well-known mimic and music hall comedian. Of late years poor Chaplin was not so fortunate, and good engagements, we are afraid, did not often come in his way. Mr Chaplin was removed to St. Thomas's Hospital suffering from dropsy, from which malady he died on Tuesday evening.[8]

The widow called round for poor Chaplin's effects. Among the blood-spotted clothing was a pair of plaid slippers with oranges stuck in the toes. She removed the fruit and a half-sovereign fell on the bed. But the legacy of Charles Chaplin was greater than any coin. He gave his son poverty and hunger, ignorance and illness, and with those things the spirit to rise above them. He gave his son the key to the clouds: showbusiness, the two-way escape. For the audience, escape from the immediate misery of life; for the performer, escape from that same misery and more, the misery of labour.

So father was dead; now mother went mad. Hannah Chaplin was put in Cane Hill Asylum for eighteen months. Syd was away at sea, so Charlie chopped wood for cheese rinds, ran errands for a soap chandler, emptied urine for a doctor. When the doctor got married, Charlie became his pageboy – a real life Buttons – but was sacked when his mistress found him blowing an iron pipe like a trumpet. A typical Chaplin improvization and a lesson for the learning: what will make 'em laugh on one side of the footlights won't make 'em laugh on the other. So Master Charles Chaplin opted out of reality: he returned to the stage. He signed on with Blackmore's Theatrical Agency. It was a conscious step upward: there would be no more clogging.

Within the month the boy was interviewed by C. E. Hamilton at the London office of the American impresario, Charles Frohman. There was an opening for a bright boy coming up in the autumn. Meanwhile would Master Chaplin care to call upon Mr H. A. Saintsbury at the Green Room Club? Master Chaplin cared, and called with some trepidation, for Saintsbury was a star. He had ambitions to be a playwright,

Cardboard Charlie

Dancing puppet made in the thirties, still sold in the seventies

too, and his latest attempt was about to be launched. Saintsbury would play Roydon Carstairs, amnesiac aristocrat, while Dorothea Desmond took the title role in *Jim: A Romance of Cockayne*. The play opened at the Royal Court Theatre, Kingston-upon-Thames on Monday, 6 July 1903; it closed at the Grand Theatre, Fulham on Saturday the eighteenth. But the boy actor not only pocketed two weeks' wages at £2. 10s a week, more money than he had ever had in his life, he also pocketed his first press cutting.

> Of the others taking part in the play, mention should be made of . . . Master Charles Chaplin, who, as a newsboy known as Sam, showed promise.[12]

Seven days later *The Era* gave Master Charles another review to clip, written by an equally anonymous correspondent from Fulham:

> Master Charles Chaplin is a broth of a boy as Sam, the newspaper boy, giving a most realistic picture of the cheeky, honest, loyal, self-reliant, philosophic street Arab who haunts the regions of Cockayne.[13]

Master Charles Chaplin was already type-cast: as himself! But read the review again. Each of the adjectives the critic applied to the boy Chaplin's 'Sam' will in ten years apply to the man Chaplin's 'Charlie'. With one exception – although as he matured Charlie even turned honest!

Master Charles now had one week in which to learn his part for *Sherlock Holmes*, the play written by the American actor, William Gillette. He was to play 'Billy', the detective's boy – another 'Buttons' – and he learned his lines as he had learned those for 'Sam'. Syd taught them to him; Charlie was still teaching himself to read. The tour opened at the Pavilion Theatre on Monday, 27 July, 1903, with Saintsbury as Holmes, and there was another cutting for the scrapbook. 'The part of Billy is well played by Mr Charles Chaplin, who succeeds in making the smart pageboy a prime favourite with the audience.'[14] It became a habit with *The Era* to mention him whenever they found room for a local review, right down to his last bow at the Royal West London Theatre on 11 June 1904: 'Master Charles Chaplin was an especial favourite as the wide-awake, quick-witted boy Billy'. On tour with him from the Christmas week at Dewsbury (Saintsbury's 500th performance as Holmes) was Sydney Chaplin. He was 18 years old and played the part of Count Von Stahlberg.

Kenneth Rivington, who had played Dr Watson, was now promoted to Holmes himself, as the star of Frohman's Midland Company. Master Charles joined him as Billy, concluding the tour at the New Theatre, Ealing, in the spring of 1905. Harry Yorke, proprietor of the Theatre Royal, Blackburn,

Poster for *The Gold Rush* released in 1925, reissued in 1942 promptly bought the rights for a cut-price tour of the smaller towns. Yorke produced, while Master Charles, the only member of the cast with experience in the Number One Company, was eager to advise on cues and stage business. This did not make the sixteen year old youth particularly popular with the more mature members of the cast. But it did give him his first taste of direction, and he liked it. When the tour reached the Court Theatre, Warrington, on 25 September 1905, a telegram was waiting: could Mr Chaplin return to London where a part awaited him in a playlet to be produced at the Duke of York's Theatre. It was signed William Postance, stage manager to William Gillette. (Chaplin thought his name was Postant, and calls him this in his autobiography. He also called him Postant in *Limelight*.)

The Painful Predicament of Sherlock Holmes, 'A Fantasy in about One-Tenth of an Act', had been written by Gillette as an answer to his critics. The American actor had returned to London to star in his own play, *Clarice*. Comments on it had been harsh, and on his accent harsher. His reply was this ten-minute skit which contrived to make Gillette the protagonist without his uttering a word. He, of course, was Holmes and Chaplin, of course, was Billy. But even the box-office lure of a double bill failed to save *Clarice*. She came off on 14 October and the curtain-raiser, twelve performances old, went with her. But by the following Tuesday Gillette and Chaplin were back in harness. The old reliable had been trotted out, and with Rivington back as Watson no more than one day's rehearsal was needed before the Duke of York's opened again with *Sherlock Holmes*.

Where *Clarice* had failed, *Sherlock* succeeded. Prince Arthur of Connaught took a party to the opening night. He clearly enjoyed it, for one month later the Duke and Duchess of Connaught went, too. So did Her Majesty Queen Alexandra, who took three royal children and the King of Greece. The play only closed because *Peter Pan* was booked in. Marie Doro, the beautiful young actress who had played the ill-fated Clarice and Sherlock's Alice, went back to the States with Gillette. With her she took the heart of the teenage Charles. A hopeless love it seemed to the youth; neither could know that given a decade both would meet on a par as Hollywood movie stars.

Sherlock Holmes took to the road again opening at the Grand, Doncaster, on New Year's Day, 1906. But nine weeks later there appeared in *The Stage* under the classification 'Professional Cards':

Charlie makes a mess

Karno comedy from stage to screen: above *Repairs* (1906) below *Work* (1915)

> Master Charles Chaplin
> *Sherlock Holmes* Co.
> Disengaged March 5th.
> Coms. 9 Tavistock Place. Tele., 2, 187 Hop.[15]

For two months Master Charles 'rested', then –

> I, the guardian of Charles Chaplin, agree for him
> to appear in *Casey's Court* wherever it may be booked
> in the British Isles only, the agreement to commence
> May 14th, 1906, at a salary weekly of £2.5.0 (two
> pounds five shillings) increasing to £2.10.0 the week
> commencing July 1906.
>
> Signed, Sydney Chaplin.

It was the first contract ever signed on Chaplin's behalf: he had just passed his seventeenth birthday, while Sydney had come of age. The week Charles opened in his new engagement, Syd was walloping whitewash in Wal Pink's slapstick sketch, *Repairs*. Although contracted for *Casey's Court*, in fact Chaplin never appeared in that famous and long-running production. He was in the sequel.

> Harry Cardle's Casey Court Companies
> Enormous Success of New Production
> THE CASEY CIRCUS
> a street urchin's idea of producing an
> up-to-date circus entertainment.
> WILL MURRAY as MRS CASEY
> Already inundated with offers.
> Sole agents: Cardle's Agency, 105, Strand.

The advertisement appeared in *The Era* on Saturday, 19 May 1906, two days before the first performance at the Olympia, Liverpool. Such was the confidence of Harry Cardle. Master Charles Chaplin, boy actor, who had trod the boards with Gillette and Saintsbury, and who had performed before crowned heads, had less confidence. *The Casey Circus* was, in his eyes, a comedown, even though his money had come up. Large as his ego had grown, he was secretly pleased that the Casey Court 'Nibs' received no individual billing.

The *Era* review of the Casey company's first London appearance at the Richmond Theatre, 6 August 1906, said 'the fun reaches its height when a burlesque imitation of "lightning cures on a poor working man" is given'. Without knowing it, they were complimenting Chaplin. Harry Cardle's conception of burlesque was elementary. For him and for his audiences it was enough to see little kids aping their elders' mannerisms and wearing their outsize clothes. This was not good enough for Chaplin, whose roots were short but in 'the legit'. (He told a Hollywood interviewer years later, 'I owe more to the tutelage of a Mr Saintsbury, who gave me my first legitimate engagement, than to anybody in the world'.) Thus, when Cardle cast Chaplin as 'Dr Body', a burlesque on Bodie the Electrical Wizard, Chaplin applied a pro's technique. He hied himself to a theatre where the star was appearing and studied his subject at first hand.

'Doctor' Walford Bodie was the greatest sensation of a sensation-loving age. All top hat, tails, and waxed moustachios, he claimed to cure cripples at every performance, thanks to the application of the latest wonder, Electricity. The man was almost a burlesque in himself, and would have brought easy laughs for Chaplin in Cardle's simplified characterization. With natural cunning, Chaplin let Cardle think he was taking direction, while secretly working on his impersonation. Chaplin would present a character study *à la* Bransby Williams, not a caricature. On opening night he dodged past the alarmed Cardle and stepped onto the stage – half a minute too soon!

'I advanced slowly, impressively, feeling the gaze of the crowd, and, with a carefully studied gesture, hung my cane – I held it by the wrong end! Instead of hanging on my arm as I expected, it clattered on the stage. Startled, I stooped to pick it up, and my high silk hat fell from my head. I grasped it, put it on quickly, and paper wadding falling out, I found my whole head buried in its black depths.'[2] A great burst of laughter came from the audience. Chaplin pushed back his topper and continued to declaim his lines with desperate seriousness. 'The more serious I was, the funnier it struck the audience.' At last his scene ended, and he came off – to such applause that he took his first return bow. 'I had stumbled on the secret of being funny, unexpectedly. An idea, going in one direction, meets an opposite idea suddenly. "Ha! Ha!" you shriek. It works every time.'

The Casey Circus ended its tour at Sadler's Wells, London, on Saturday 20 July, 1907. The following Monday a new production took the road, *Casey's Army*. Charles Chaplin was not in the cast. Syd, travelling the country with a Fred Karno company, kept an eye out for his kid brother. The Karno organization was so large that it was only a matter of time before a vacancy would occur.

Fred Karno was the comedy king of England, the most powerful force for fun in the Edwardian world. His ribald repertory had spread throughout the land and over the seas, where his greatest success, the legendary *Mumming Birds*, wowed them in Paris as it did on the Bowery. Born Westcott in Exeter on 26 March 1866, Fred the plumber's mate rose, via his hobby, gymnastics, to become purveyor of pantomime to all classes. *Jail Birds, Early Birds, Mumming Birds:* one by one the slapstick sketches hatched from Fred's Fun Factory, as he called his home, Hilarity Villa, 28 Vaughan Road, Loughborough Junction, S.E. And out of this slapstick academy, the original school of hard knocks, came the funniest men on the music halls. Flatfooted Fred Kitchen ('Meredith, we're in!'); wistful, whistling Harry Weldon ('S'no use!'); Billy Reeves the Tipsy Swell, and a rising young comic called Syd Chaplin, who played Billy's part in the States when American demand

Charlie pulls the Chain

The Champion (1916) with Leo White

22

for Karno comedy grew so great that Fred had to ship out a second company.

And Charles Chaplin, whom Karno did not particularly want. 'Syd brought his kid brother along, a pale, puny, sullen-looking youngster. I must say that when I first saw him, I thought he looked much too shy to do any good in the theatre, particularly in the knockabout comedies that were my speciality.'[17] But 'The Guv'nor' gave in to Syd's persistent pressings and let the lad try when a spot fell vacant in his current tour of *London Suburbia*. 'The first scene, which shows three villas, displays the everyday life with its attendant distractions in the shape of butchers, coalmen, greengrocers, street singers, and German bands.'[18] *The Era* failed to mention one 'attendant distraction': a rag-and-bone man, played by Charles Chaplin. But if the critics did not notice him, the Guv'nor did. Karno promised him a better part when the time came. And it did, five months later.

The Football Match was Karno's biggest production. Harry Weldon led the field as Stiffy the Goalkeeper; the comedian who played the villain is imprecisely recorded, and perhaps this is significant, for Karno decided to replace him with Charles Chaplin. At the end of January, 1908 Weldon reluctantly took time off from golf for two quick run-throughs with the new man. And on Monday, 3 February, they opened at the London Coliseum, a not unimportant date in the music hall book.

The curtain rose on the Training Quarters of the Muddleton Piecans at a pub called The Bull. As such it was equipped with the gymnastic apparatus so beloved by acrobatic Karno. Enter Chaplin, clad in voluminous Inverness cape, immaculate in top hat and spats; and enter Chaplin with his back to the audience. It was an old theatrical dodge learned from Saintsbury, but it was new to the vaudeville stage. He wheeled on the audience and showed them the twist: the dapper dude sported a scarlet nose! Then came another stage in the basic Chaplin formula, the destruction of dignity. The upperclass toff's downfall was brought about by his own symbol, the swaggering whangee cane. It tangled with a springy punchbag, smacking him in the head. The consequent stagger prompted another instant gag: the stick swung up to slap his cheek. As the laughter built it spurred Chaplin into that special stream-of-unconsciousness creativity that was his own. By the time Weldon made his entrance the audience was thoroughly warmed up. After the show the star's approval of the new member was grudging but given; by the end of the tour his feelings were expressed in deeds rather than words: the stage slap he gave Chaplin's cheek drew blood.

Karno had signed his new find to a twelve month contract at four pounds a week, so in June, when *The Football Match* was played out, he sent Chaplin to perform at the Folies Bergères in Paris. Karno had founded his companies in the nineties when dialogue was still banned on the music hall stage. His first troupe had been billed as Karno's Speechless Comedians, and this pantomime tradition was strongly maintained. It held them in good stead when European engagements came their way. All comedy dialogue was dropped in favour of fully visual sketches, and the most famous of these was the appropriately titled *Mumming Birds*. It was in this piece, in Paris, that the nineteen year old Chaplin perfected the wordless pantomime that would prove the making of his fame and fortune in the

Charlie in the Comics

First appearance of Chaplin as a comic strip hero, drawn by Bertie Brown.

CHARLIE CHAPLIN APPEARS TO-DAY. CHARLIE CHAPLIN

The Funny Wonder

½d

VOL. II.—No. 72.]   EVERY TUESDAY.   [WEEK ENDING AUGUST 7, 1915.

CHARLIE CHAPLIN, the Scream of the Earth (*the famous Essanay Comedian*).

1. Here he is, readers! Good old Charlie! Absolutely IT! A scream from start to finish. What's he doing now, eh? "Twas here," says he, standing in a graceful posish, by an artistically designed coal-hole, with the faithful hound attached to his cane: "'Twas here I was to meet Maggie! Phwpsts!" But see! A rival approaches!

2. Then the rival, one Esmond MacSydeslyppe Hugo Balscadden O'Chuckitupp—the rival, we repeat, did a bit of dirty work. Fact! He held forth a tempting bone, and Charlie's faithful hound cast the eye of approval on same. Base rival! "Soon," says the chirpy Charlie, putting on another fag: "Soon she will be here. Oh, joy!"

3. But the hound, deciding to do the chew on the bone, legged it up the paving stones, taking Charlie's stick with him. And Charlie, with his visible means of support thus removed, did a graceful flop into said coal-hole just as the lovely Maggie appeared! "Charlie!" said she, with much spurnery, "What do you think you're doing?"

4. Ha! Enter the rival! "Don't you have anything to do with him, Maggie," says the rival: "He's absolutely sale price, he is. Marked down to one-and-nine-three-him! Come with me to some nook, where we may hold converse!"

5. So off they went to the nook, but Charlie was soon up and doing. Yea! He flopped along, soon coming upon the rival telling the tale of love to the beauteous one. "Ho!" says he. "Now to get a portion of my own back! Now for it!"

6. Well, the rival was just on the point of laying his riches at the damsel's dainty patent number two's, when Charlie, picking up a dustbin (full flavour) which happened to be handy, shoved it into his outstretched fins. Which did it—yes!

7. Up jumped the young person. Talk about the frozen eye! Wow! "Sir-r!" she said: "I did not come here to be entertained by such poltroonery. Please remove yourself forthwith. Your face causes me uneasiness! No explanations, please! Get hence and proceed to climb trees for mushrooms. All is over between us!"—Or words to that effect. Then Charlie did the inward chuckle, and raised his hat with courtly grace.

8. And he did the affable and endearing chat that completely restored him to favour in the damsel's eyes. "Permit me to suggest," says this gallant old filbert, "a light lunch at the Café de Chanceitt, with a jaunt on the merry old motor-'bus to follow. Having just received my quarterly allowance—not half—all is well. Let us proceed!" And they did proceed—some! More news next week, so look out!

brave new art form of the twentieth century, the silent cinema.

Mumming Birds had originally opened on 13 June 1904; it would run around the world for forty years. The comedians changed; only the structure stayed the same. The original script filled one foolscap sheet; the rest was improvization. It was a show-within-a-show, a burlesque variety entertainment continually interrupted by members of the 'audience', principally a boy who threw food from the O.P. box, and a drunk who persistently joined in from the prompt side. The turns included an Extempore Topical Singer, an utterly indistinct Ballad Singer, an inept conjurer, and the climactic act, Marconi the Terrible Turkey, prepared to wrestle all comers for £25. The drunk of course took up the challenge, downed the Turk, and claimed the prize. The show concluded with a typical Karno climax: 'A general mêlée ensues and the curtains close on an uproarious scene'. The Inebriated Swell, as the original programme called him, was Billy Reeves: 'A finer example of the dazed condition due to an advanced stage of drunkenness we have not seen on the variety stage'.[19] It was Reeves who first played the Drunk in America, and whom the young Chaplin saw before he ever dreamed he would become a Karno comic himself. It was Reeves whom Chaplin was hired to emulate on that Paris tour, and it was Reeves' brother Alfred who acted as producer-manager to both Billy's and Chaplin's American tours. And it was Alf Reeves who became Chaplin's own manager in the movies.

At the end of his first year with Karno, his contract was renewed and Chaplin worked his way through the Guv'nor's comedy compendium, travelling round and round the Moss and Stoll circuits with the 'B' company versions of Fred Kitchen's *The G.P.O.*, Billy Reeves' *Mumming Birds*, Gus Le Clerq's *The Yap-Yaps*, and his brother's own *Skating*, a skit on the rinking craze of 1909. At last Karno offered the rising star a sketch of his own, *Jimmy the Fearless; or, The Boy 'Ero*, written by Charles Baldwin and F. O'Neill. Chaplin read it, and turned it down. Karno, brooking no nonsense from swelling heads, promptly put it on with another of his up-and-coming comedians, Stanley Jefferson. Chaplin went to see it, changed his mind, and called on Karno. The following Monday, 25 April 1910, the cast list of the sketch at the Stratford Empire was headed: 'Jimmy . . . Mr Charles Chaplin'.

Chaplin, just turned twenty-one, was still slight and slender enough to pass as the kind of cocky, Cockney kid he had played with Gillette. Home long past the permitted hour, ('I've been out with a bit o' skirt'), he cheeked his parents and sliced his own supper, improvizing business with the bread that brought applause. Then, diving into his favourite Penny Dreadful, he dozed off into a dream sequence that formed the bulk of the action. 'The scene is transferred to a saloon of a settler's camp

Charlie in the New World: 1913

Poster for Sullivan and Considine's Empress.

Also appearing: May Reeves, Alf Reeves, and Stanley Jefferson

in the wild west; . . . a lovely maiden is kidnapped and brought in by the bushranger chief, and is rescued single-handed by the valiant Jimmy, who subsequently, with the aid of friendly redskins, vanquishes the robbers, in addition to defeating their chief in a duel of swords.' He returns home rich in time to save his old folks from eviction, but then comes the twist. Wrathful father wakes him from his dream, 'puts the would-be hero across his knee, and soundly trounces him'.[20]

This tour ended on 3 September at the Empire, Bradford. One month later, on 3 October, Chaplin opened at the Colonial Theatre, New York, U.S.A. The show was *The Wow-Wows*, written by Herbert Sydney as a sequel to *The Yap-Yaps*, and Chaplin starred as the Hon. Archibald Binks. He had seen Syd play the part, and considered the sketch 'silly, fatuous, and without merit';[1] but he eagerly agreed to take on the tour for the chance of a trip to the States.

Scene One showed a crowd of campers cooking breakfast 'in the way beloved of farce writers'. Archie pockets an egg, and promptly smashes it while kneeling to declare his love for a lady visitor. She asks him if he enjoyed his bathe. 'Did the water come up to your expectations?' 'No', says Archie. 'It only reached my knees!' Saucy dialogue was succeeded by saucy sights, and *The Era* was shocked by 'an alleged witch putting on a pair of stays, which are drawn up over the legs.'[21] On Chaplin's American tour, the legs thus exposed belonged to Muriel Palmer. Also in his company was Whimsical Walker, an ageing clown from Drury Lane, and Stanley Jefferson. Like Chaplin, both would find fame in the films: Walker for Cecil M. Hepworth under the name of Jamie Darling, Jefferson for Hal E. Roach under the name of Stan Laurel. *The Wow-Wows* was a success despite Chaplin's forebodings. *Variety*, bible of the Biz, wrote:

> Chaplin is typically English, the sort of comedian that the American audiences seem to like, although unaccustomed to. His manner is quiet and easy, and he goes about his work in a devil-may-care manner, in direct contrast to the twenty-minutes-from-a-cemetary makeup he employs. Chaplin will do all right for America.[21]

After a twenty week tour across the continent on the Sullivan and Considine circuit, William Morris gave the company six weeks at his American Theatre on 42nd Street and 8th Avenue. Legend goes that in the audience on the night Chaplin did his drunk in *A Night in an English Music Hall* (as *Mumming Birds* was called in the States) he was seen by a pair of up-and-coming comedians from the movies. 'If ever I become a big shot, there's a guy I'll sign up', said the man to the girl. They were from the American Mutoscope and Biograph Company, and their names were Mack Sennett and Mabel Normand.

KEYSTONE

3
His
New Profession
(1913-1914)

THE KEYSTONE FILM CO.

Charlie in the Park

Getting Acquainted (1914)
with Mabel Normand,
Phyllis Allen and Mack
Swain

12 May 1913

Alf Reeves, Manager,
Karno Company,
Nixon Theatre,
Philadelphia, Pa.
Is there a man named Chaffin in your
company or something like that stop
if so will he communicate with Kessel
and Baumann 24 Longacre Building
Broadway New York

Charles Chaffin or something like that took the early train for New York, full of excitement. Longacre Building was a reputed hive of lawyers: maybe a rich relation had died and left him a fortune? In fact, there was a fortune awaiting him, but at the time the offer of 125 dollars a week for 52 weeks did little to prolong Chaplin's excitement. Adam Kessel Jr and Charles O. Baumann were not lawyers, but partners in the New York Motion Picture Company. Their product was divided into four brands: Kay-Bee (named after the owners' initials), Broncho (for westerns), Domino (for dramas) and Keystone (for comedies). It seemed that their Mr Mack Sennett, director of productions for the Keystone branch, was in need of a new comedian for his thrice-weekly releases. He had asked them to locate 'the man who played the drunk in the box'. The offer was good, double what Chaplin was getting from Karno, but still he hesitated. He had seen Keystone comedies and was not enamoured of their frantic rough-and-tumble. He wished his big brother was there to handle the situation, and considered what Syd would have done. He did it: he asked for 200 dollars. Mr Kessel said he would let him know. Chaplin went back on the road, wondering if he had made a terrible mistake. At last a letter came. Keystone were offering Chaplin more money than he had ever earned in his life: 150 dollars a week for the first three months, 175 a week for the next nine. He accepted by return.

Mack Sennett's first doubts about his new find occurred when he called backstage at the Empress, Los Angeles, after a performance of *A Night in a London Club*. As Sennett and Chaplin talked face to face for the first time, the decrepit old drunk creamed off his makeup to reveal a 24-year old man who looked eight years younger. While Chaplin finished his tour, Sennett had several weeks to worry whether his hunch had been right. Maybe this Chaffin chap was too raw for the daily grind of movie-making, Keystone style. The Karno tour closed at Kansas City on Saturday 28 November 1913. Without knowing it, the Empress Theatre audience that night witnessed Charles Chaplin's last regular live performance. Arthur Dando, who had been with Chaplin since *Jimmy the Fearless*, made a presentation on behalf of the company. It was a tangible demonstration of how he, and they, felt about Chaplin's success. When he opened the package Chaplin found a battered tobacco tin containing stubs of old greasepaint.

Mack Sennett was the Karno of the kinematograph, a creator of comedy for his modern age. Where Karno produced slap-stick sketches and sent them round the theatres, Sennett produced them, photographed them and sent them round the cinemas. But where Karno could get by on at most six new shows a year, Sennett had to turn them out at the rate of six new films a fortnight. His Fun Factory, like Karno's, was situated in the suburbs and, like Karno's, had expanded through success into a sprawling site. When Chaplin took his first street-car ride to Glendale, the sight that met his eyes as he walked up Allesandro Street to number 1712 was anything but reassuring.

'A glare of light and heat burst upon me. The stage, a yellow board floor covering at least two blocks, lay in a blaze of sunlight intensified by dozens of white canvas reflectors stretched overhead. On it was a wilderness of "sets" – drawing rooms, prison interiors, laundries, balconies, staircases, caves, fire escapes, kitchens, cellars. Hundreds of actors were strolling about in costume; carpenters were hammering away at new sets; five companies were playing before five clicking cameras. There was a roar of confused sound – screams, laughs, an explosion, shouted commands, pounding, whistling, the bark of a dog. The air was thick with the smell of new lumber in the sun, flashlight powder, cigarette smoke.'[2]

Edendale was Camberwell, Keystone was Karno, but amplified a thousandfold. And so was Chaplin's loneliness. Never a mixer, always alone save for a close crony or so, he felt utterly isolated in the chaos of Keystone. Chester Conklin, a Sennett support who sported soulful eyes and a drooping moustache, spotted the shy little newcomer and took him to lunch. Chaplin, eager to talk, began to boast about his salary: 'I'm going to save it carefully and very soon I shall be able to return to England with a tidy bankroll.'[22] At two o'clock Chaplin reported to his director. 'Is it an acrobatic part?' he enquired nervously, having just seen a Keystone comic fall twenty-five feet into a net that broke. The director reassured him. All he had to do was to take a pie out of his pocket, hear a noise, put the pie down, and turn back to discover rats nibbling it. Chaplin rehearsed the scene, but each time he got out of the range of the camera lens. The director got the 'Props' to paint a circle of white dots on the floor, and with this as his footlights, Chaplin perfected the scene. He was sent to the communal dressing-room to make up. In early movies theatrical tradition maintained: actors did their own makeup. Chaplin created his character with care, remembering Sennett had found his face looked too youthful. When he returned to the set the director threw a fit. 'Look at your skin, man; it will register gray – and those lines – you can't use lines like that in the pictures!

Charlie meets the Movie Makers: 1914

Thomas Ince, Mack Sennett, David Wark Griffith

Roberts, go show him how to make up.'[2] The new boy, thoroughly humiliated in front of crew and company, was led back to the dressing room where he had his face painted over brick-brown and his eyelashes loaded with heavy black. The director approved and the camera turned on Chaplin's first film.

It was a disaster. First Chaplin was unnerved by the clicking of the camera. Then the instructions shouted by the director took his mind off any hope of characterization or improvization. Every tumble took him out of camera range. The director was furious; used to working with professionals, and proud of his one-take record, here he was running up a bill for exposed footage that he knew would be impossible to use. At last the light failed and he called it a day. Chaplin knew he had failed; nobody had laughed at him, and when he saw the film in company with Sennett he seemed unfunnier than ever. He had a black face and a white moustache: to save costs the film was shown in negative.

'Funny? A blind man couldn't have laughed at it. I had ironed out any trace of humor in the scenario. I was stiff, wooden, stupid. I felt as though the whole thing were a horrible nightmare of shame and embarrassment.'[2] Fortunately for Chaplin, unfortunately for posterity, his first film was never shown to the public. Now Sennett was really worried. He had a get-out clause in Chaplin's contract, but his mistake could still cost him twelve times 150 dollars. Crossing his fingers he gave Chaplin a week to find his feet, observe how pictures were made, watch actors and directors in action. Chaplin took nearly three before he felt ready, or perhaps obliged, to try again.

It was a favourite format of the Sennett school to use actual events and interesting locations to add colour to their comedies. Reed Heustis, the scenario editor, had concocted a plot around the machine room of the *Los Angeles Times*, and the script, or what passed for one at Keystone, was passed over to Henry Lehrman. 'Pathé' Lehrman, as he had been nicknamed since the day he had talked D. W. Griffith into hiring him by pretending he was an expert from Paris, was the king of this kind of picture. He could take a cameraman and a couple of actors and whip up a comedy before lunch, directing, writing, and playing the lead to boot. More than any other man, Lehrman was responsible for the action-packed, breakneck style of movie-making that the world still calls Keystone Comedy. Lehrman was no respecter of personalities, let alone the more leisurely ways of Karno comedy as practised by Charles Chaplin. And so, with an experienced and unsympathetic director who not only shouted orders at him from behind the camera but also played the hero in front, Chaplin was confused enough without the piecemeal approach of cinematic construction.

'The interiors were all played on the stage, and most of the exteriors were taken "on location". It was most confusing, after being booted through a door, to be obliged to appear on the other side of it, two days later, with the same expression, and complete the tumble begun fifteen miles away. It was still more confusing to play the scenes in reverse order, and I ruined three hundred feet of film by losing my hat at the end of a scene, when the succeeding one had already been played with my hat on.'[2]

The hat in question was a tall silk topper, and with it Chaplin wore an Oxford grey cutaway frock-coat, a check waistcoat, a stiff batwing collar, a polka-dot cravat, and walrus whiskers. Complete with monocle and walking cane he was the classic conception of the English dude he had played on stage for years. But Charlie quickly reveals himself as a phoney when he touches a passer-by (Lehrman) for a handout. Immediately he begins to flirt with the nearest female (Virginia Kirtley): he kisses her hand, then races his pursed lips up her arm!

'When we started I could see that Lehrman was groping for ideas. And of course being a newcomer at Keystone I was anxious to make suggestions. This was where I created antagonism with Lehrman. In a scene in which I had an interview with an editor of a newspaper, I crammed in every conceivable gag I could think of, even to suggesting business for others in the cast.'[1]

Charlie on Wheels
Making a Living (1914)
Mabel at the Wheel (1914)

When he saw the final cut of the film in company with Sennett and Lehrman, Chaplin's worst fears were realized. 'I was stiff; I took all the surprise out of the scenes by anticipating the next motion. When I walked against a tree, I showed that I knew I would hit it, long before I did. I was so determined to be funny that every muscle in my body was stiff and serious with the strain.'[2] Then there was the editing: 'The cutter had butchered it beyond recognition, cutting into the middle of all my funny business.' Chaplin, bewildered, had a flaming row with Lehrman, and Sennett laid him off for yet another week. Completed before Christmas, *Making A Living* was not released to the cinemas until February 1914.

Had there been no time lag between preview and review, there might never have been 'Charlie the Tramp'. Had Chaplin and Sennett suspected that critics and customers would welcome *Making a Living*, they would have cheerfully continued the adventures of 'Charlie the Dude'. But as it was, Chaplin spent his suspension experimenting with costumes and characterisations, trying to raise a smile or two around the lot. It had become a challenge: he must make these Yankees laugh.

There came a day when not only Chaplin was laid off, Chester Conklin and co. were, too. The reason was rain. Unable to take the locations for *Mabel's Strange Predicament*,

they were holed up in the communal dressing-room playing pinochle. Chaplin ambled in. They already knew better than to ask him to join them; Chaplin's meanness with money, a care born of poverty, was already legendary at the studio. Roscoe Arbuckle, the funny fat man, had left his trousers over a chair. Chaplin fingered them and pulled them on. People smiled. Charles Avery's coat was handy, so Chaplin put that on. Avery was even smaller than Chaplin, and so his coat-tails jutted out over the bunched-up bottom of the Arbuckle pants. A chuckle was heard. Mr Durfee's derby was on a peg. Chaplin took it down and made it flutter over his head, from behind. Somebody laughed. Mack Swain's moustache, the one he wore in his character of 'Ambrose', was on the shelf. Chaplin stuck it on, then trimmed it down until he could wiggle it just like the fellow he had watched so closely the night before, who had supped soup so twitchily it had made him laugh. Now Chaplin's twitches made Sennett's boys laugh. The brown brogues belonged to Ford Sterling, the star of the studio. Curled at the toes, they were so large on Chaplin's tiny feet that the only way they would stay on was to reverse their order, left on right. Thus accidental expediency helped evolve the most famous walk in the world.

Chaplin had created Charlie. But there was more than instant inspiration in the character he came to call 'The Little Fellow'. There was a lifetime of observation. Truth behind the comic surface put warmth in the laughter of his colleagues that rainy day sixty years ago, when the Tramp was born of whole if shabby cloth; a warmth that would bring a responsive glow from audiences all over the world. And particularly from Chaplin's old teacher at Victory Place: 'He copied his famous walk from an old man who gave oatmeal and water to the horses in cabs and carts outside the Elephant and Castle.'[10] Today, in the concrete and glass complex that stands where that old man once stood, is a bright new pub. It is called 'The Charlie Chaplin'.

Mack Sennett looked in the dressing-room to see what his boys were laughing at. He saw Charlie the Tramp, shuffling and strutting, shrugging and smirking, swinging his whangee cane (Chaplin's favourite hand-prop since the Karno days), and generally kicking up the laughs with whatever met his hand or eye. Sennett joined in the laughter and ended the suspension, sending Chaplin to the boardwalk at nearby Venice where a soapbox derby was about to be run. The annual home-made car race for kids was ideal stuff for a Keystone quickie, and would make a perfect proving ground for Chaplin's new character. Sennett only hoped that the personal antagonism between Chaplin and Lehrman would not spoil the film. Next morning the Keystone crew arrived at Venice: Chaplin, Lehrman, ace cameraman Frank D. Williams, and four of the Keystone kids, pint-size professionals who knew how to play in front of the camera. Forty-five minutes later the film was complete and in the can.

Kid Auto Races at Venice is pure Chaplin impromptu. A contemporary critic's attempt at a synopsis still holds good: 'The funny man enters into the spirit of the meeting and persistently obstructs the cameramen in their operations.'[24] No more can be said, or need be. Charlie, apparently screen-struck, pesters and postures, stealing the scene. Sennett was delighted. He had discovered the key to Chaplin's comedy. He needed time to let the gags occur, develop and flow. Next day Lehrman took up *Mabel's Strange Predicament* where rain had stopped play. He found an addition to his original cast, Charles Chaplin. His reaction may be gauged by the credit the film carries: directed by Henry Lehrman and Mack Sennett.

For the first time in films Chaplin played his classic stage drunk. He ad-libbed around the lobby of an hotel set. 'I entered and stumbled over the foot of a lady. I turned and raised my hat apologetically, then turned and stumbled over a cuspidor, then turned and raised my hat to the cuspidor. Behind the camera they began to laugh.'[1] This was the very thing Chaplin had missed in movies: the living laughter of an audience. The cold clicking eye of the camera froze his creative mind; he needed the two-way contact of laughter to trigger the flow of jokes. The lobby scene became Chaplin's scene; it ran seven times longer than the Keystone norm. Lehrman wanted to cut it but found he couldn't: Chaplin had quickly learned how to outwit 'the butchers'. He introduced gags at his entrance and exit which virtually sealed him into the sequence. Chaplin stole the scene, but not the picture; that remained firmly in the fair hands of its star, Mabel of the Strange Predicament.

If Mack Sennett was the founding father of American film comedy, then Mabel Normand was its mother, albeit a young one. But seventeen when she left Biograph to help Mack form Keystone, she had already knocked up a two year career in comedies. Her big-eyed, buxom, bubbling beauty – five feet of fun – won the hearts of millions who called her 'Keystone Mabel'. She was a star, and more, she was the boss's girl. Mack was fifteen years her senior and would break her heart, but meanwhile they worked and played in perfect harmony and there was no room for the handsome young Englishman except as a Keystone colleague. Mabel had been in on Chaplin's discovery from the start, and generously gave of her time to help him settle into cinema. She gave him more: style. Samuel Peeples, film maker and historian, has found that 'a study of her films made before Chaplin came to this country, shows entire routines, gestures, reactions, expressions, that were later a part of Chaplin's characterisations.'[25]

The rain had stopped, but great puddles flooded the gutters of Glendale. Inspired by the sight, Lehrman and Williams set forth on another improvization. The result was *Between*

above: *Kid Auto Races at Venice* (1914), with Henry Lehrman.

Chaplin wears his tramp outfit for the first time in films.

right: Charlie's Costume

Charlie's Skid
Laughing Gas (1914)

Showers: Charlie the Tramp acting Raleigh to Emma Clifton's stranded Elizabeth. He takes the chance for a spot of flirtation, establishing a curious characteristic of the Tramp: despite his shabbiness he is utterly irresistible to the opposite sex (a characteristic, perhaps, of Chaplin himself). The flirtation is striking: for the first time in films it is carried out with the protagonist's back to the camera, a trick of the 'legit' absorbed into the Chaplin repertoire in the days of Saintsbury.

Charlie's rival Raleigh is a grimacing grotesque in a goatee. This is Ford Sterling, Chaplin's rival in more ways than one. It was an on-screen echo of off-screen conflict. Sterling, Sennett's star since their Biograph days, was working out his Keystone contract. Sennett had made Sterling's spastic Dutchman world famous, and naturally Sterling wanted a rise. Sennett refused, so Sterling signed with Universal. This was the reason Sennett had played a hunch and hired Chaplin. *Between Showers* was to introduce his new star alongside his old. But now Sennett was shocked to discover that the film would be the last to be made for him by his long-time partner, Henry Lehrman. He had signed with Universal, too.

Chaplin, at least, was pleased to see Lehrman leave. He hoped for a little more understanding from whichever Keystone director he would be assigned to next. It turned out to be George Nichols, a man who had been in pictures since their beginning, and who was now approaching sixty. 'I had the same trouble with him', wrote Chaplin. Nevertheless he managed to slip several spontaneities into *A Film Johnnie*, a plot which the new scenario editor, Craig Hutchinson, had concocted around the Keystone Studio itself. Charlie visits a nickelodeon and falls violently in love with the pretty star on the screen. Ejected for creating a disturbance, he heads for the studio to see Virginia Kirtley in person. He gets in by posing as an actor, and echoing his pest of *Kid Auto Races*, promptly ruins the film that is in production. Mack Sennett, playing himself, hears of a nearby fire, and true to Keystone custom despatches a company to the scene with orders to improvize a picture. Charlie tags along, mistakes the staged danger for the real thing, and ruins the take. They turn the firehose on him, a slapstick finale which Charlie tops by turning his ear and squirting water out of his mouth: a personal twist which refocuses the attention on the comedian instead of the comedy.

Chaplin had made five films in four weeks, but as yet his name had not appeared in print. Sennett, still uncertain, had deliberately refrained from publicizing him. The first breakthrough came when the *Moving Picture World* critic, noting the new face in Keystone comedies, and hearing on the grapevine that Sennett's latest discovery hailed from Britain, being unable to put a name to him, invented one! Reviewing *A Film Johnnie* he wrote, 'Edgar English's work in this picture will keep it amusing.'[26] Meanwhile, as may be expected, it was a British paper that was first to publish the new star's correct name. The Western Import Company, overseas distributor of Keystone productions, placed this advertisement in *The Bioscope* of 26 March 1914:

> Keystone's latest capture is Chas. Chaplin, the famous comedian of Fred Karno's *Mumming Birds* Company. Watch for him and for Mack Sennett and Mabel Normand in better-than-ever Keystones.

One such was *Tango Tangles*, a prime piece of improvization shot in a Los Angeles ballroom during a single public session. Sennett directed and all his top comics took part, Sterling, Arbuckle, Chaplin and Conklin. Only Chester sported his customary walrus; the others appeared without makeup, and good looking, suntanned young fellows they all seem. Chaplin plays his classic drunk, his youth giving the inebriation a charm lacking on the only other occasion he played drunk without makeup, in *Limelight* forty years later. 'The band leader has a sneaky feeling for the hat check girl': so does Charlie and so does Fatty the clarinettist. Soon everyone is engaged in a free-for-all fight, with Fatty doing his celebrated high kick, Ford leaping like a madman and biting Charlie's nose, and Charlie squaring up with style before flopping out with his feet up. For its glimpse of dapper Chaplin, so young, so handsome, so acrobatic, this little film is unique.

The battle which climaxed *Tango Tangles* becomes the prelude for *His Favorite Pastime*, with Charlie and Fatty slugging it out in a bar. This time Charlie is both Tramp and Drunk, and experiences his first cinematic encounters with swing doors (he capitulates and crawls underneath it) and bad smells (a stinking Limburger is planted in his pocket). He also displays his obnoxious obsession with the opposite sex, and follows pretty Peggy Pearce to her home, breaks in, and flirts with her – until he discovers his mistake. He has been trying to seduce her Negro maid! In life, Chaplin's advances to his leading lady were more successful. He and Peggy Pearce fell in love. But, as in the film, it ended unhappily. Chaplin wanted love, Peggy wanted marriage. They never appeared in a film together again. Appropriately, his next picture was called *Cruel, Cruel Love*.

This rare film was a change of pace for Chaplin. He is neither drunk nor tramp, but a man of wealth with walrus whiskers. As Mr Dovey he retains one touch of the old Charlie: he is an incorrigible flirt. Finding his fiancée away he cheerfully tackles her maid. Later the loved one spots the pair in the park and breaks the engagement. Charlie decides to end it all, but his faithful butler switches the fatal dose for water. Charlie drinks, and on his supposed death-bed sees himself in Hell (the first 'dream sequence' in Chaplin films). Then

Charlie's Back

left: *The Circus* (1928)

above: *The Idle Class* (1921)

below: *The Gold Rush* (1925)

comes his fiancée's letter of forgiveness! Stomach-pumps are summoned and the truth comes out.

Minta Durfee, the pretty little wife of Roscoe Arbuckle, played Mr Dovey's love, and she was also the landlady who favoured Charlie in his next film, *The Star Boarder*. On a country outing she tumbles from an apple tree right on top of Charlie, and the consequent confusion makes a fine study for her young son to secretly snap. A similar but less innocent scene between his father (Edgar Kennedy) and another guest is also caught by the kid's camera, and both are later displayed to the assembled guests via magic lantern. Landlord and lodger lay into one another, and the scandalmonger has an unhappy ending: he is spanked by Charlie.

The film was released on 4 April 1914, a key date in the rise of the new star, for on that day *Moving Picture World* carried the first advertisement to exploit Chaplin as a commodity. His 8 × 10 portrait was offered for sale as part of a set featuring Mack Sennett, Mabel Normand, and Roscoe Arbuckle. You got all four by sending 50 cents to the Keystone Publicity Department. Thus Chaplin was now a fully made up member of the Keystone constellation, ranking third in the heirarchy over Arbuckle, if the arrangement of this advertisement is interpreted correctly. So when George Nichols, who had made four in a row with Chaplin, went to Sennett and called the new star 'a son-of-a-bitch',[1] Sennett simply passed Chaplin on to the next director in line. This happened to be Mabel Normand. The two stars, who had been getting along famously as fellow performers, clashed immediately.

Mabel at the Wheel was to be another Keystone cash-in on a current event. The annual Vanderbilt Cup Race was about to be run. Charlie, sporting top hat, frock coat, moustache and goatee, clings to his swinging cane as if in one small particular way to avoid comparison with Ford Sterling. Harry McCoy, Charlie's rival, is driving in the race, so Charlie hires some henchmen to lock him in a shed. Mabel takes Harry's place at the wheel and despite all Charlie can do, including watering the track to make the cars skid, she wins the Cup. It was the watering scene that started the trouble. Chaplin suggested he should step on the hose, stop the water, then let it squirt into his face. Mabel rejected the gag: not, surprisingly, on the grounds of its age, but on the same factor that had so concerned Lehrman and Nichols: 'We have no time,' she said, 'do what you're told.' Chaplin, who had found this hard before, found it impossible to take from a woman, especially one younger than he. He refused, called Mabel incompetent, and sat on the kerb in a sulk. Mabel was apalled, the crew offered to beat Chaplin up, and Sennett was appealed to. He delivered an ultimatum: co-operate or quit.

Next morning Chaplin found Sennett all smiles. He would step in and personally direct the rest of the film. Chaplin

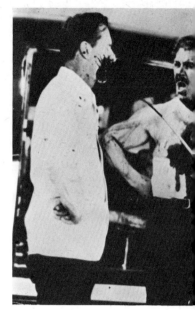

Charlie and the Squirt

above: *Modern Times* (1936)

below: *Limelight* (1952)

agreed, but only if Sennett promised him the chance to direct a film himself. Sennett concurred, and later Chaplin discovered why. Kessel and Baumann had wired from New York. Chaplin releases were making more money than any previous Keystones, and the demand was increasing every day. They wanted more Chaplins immediately. Sennett obliged, even if the only way to get them was to let Chaplin have his stubborn head. *Twenty Minutes of Love* was rushed through production and released two days after *Mabel at the Wheel*. The director was Joseph Maddern, the location Westlake Park, and the story was 'written' by Chaplin. He improvised it after the earlier *Between Showers*, substituting a watch for the much-stolen umbrella. The concluding riot lands everybody in the lake – except Charlie and his girl. Clearly Chaplin was breaking himself in as a movie-maker with standard Sennett stuff. For a first screenplay it presented nothing new. But it allowed a little more time for the star's spontaneities, as with the way he embraces a tree when he spots a spooning pair.

Chaplin's aim was direction, and he achieved it by co-direction. He mended his rift with Mabel and together they made *Caught in a Cabaret*. Charlie is no tramp, but a humble waiter at a cheap café. In his off hour he takes his dachshund to water Westlake Park, where Mabel is taking the air with her fiancé, Harry McCoy. Confronted by a crook, Harry flees, but Charlie rushes to the rescue with a few well-placed kicks to the face. He introduces himself to Mabel as the Premier of Greenland. Impressed she invites him home to meet the folks. At Mabel's place a garden party is in full swing. Charlie corners her in an arbour and the busy plot takes a breather to let Chaplin give Charlie his head. In a single scene, short but long by current Keystone standards, Charlie makes love to Mabel. Mad, improvised love, a gamut of crazy courting, with shy smiles and saucy smirks, nudges that accelerate to embraces by both arm and leg; suave cigarette smoke that chokes him and a bottle of wine that goes to his already love-drunk head. Mabel is swept off her feet by this concentrated courtship, of course. But, like Cinderella, Charlie must return to drudging reality. Cunning Harry promptly whisks Mabel and her society chums to Kennedy's café. At the awful exposure Charlie drops his pile of plates: their love and their future is smashed.

Chaplin's first full-blown, two-reel screenplay was another compromise. He coupled a Keystone custard-pie climax to a class-conscious plot that allowed passages of personal impromptu. Whilst not presenting Charlie as the Tramp, he maintained much of the Tramp's character. His lowly waiter aimed at the higher life, and was not above imposture to achieve it. There was something of the dundreary dude from his first film here, but with greater depth. Charlie was no longer the con man out for cash at any cost; he was looking for love.

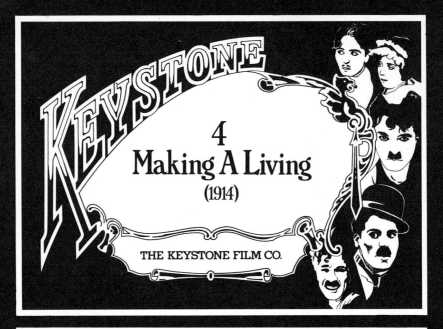

KEYSTONE

4
Making A Living
(1914)

THE KEYSTONE FILM CO.

Chaplin has created an entirely new variety of screen comedian – a weird figure in whom one may recognise elements of the dude, the tramp, the acrobat, and, flavouring all, the 'silly ass' of whom the drunken swell in *Mumming Birds* was so perfect a type. This extraordinary character wanders through the recent Keystone releases – there is no other word to describe the Chaplin touch – and indulges in escapades which are side-splitting in their weird absurdity and their amazing suddenness.

This first critical attempt to pin down Chaplin's screen personality appeared in *Kinematograph Weekly*. A thousand others would try, including Chaplin, but none would equal that paper's neat nutshell, 'the Dilapidated Knut'. Meanwhile the world's first totally-Chaplin film was made and released. He conceived it, scripted it, starred in it, directed it, and called it *Caught In The Rain*. Chaplin had staked his new career on it; more, he had staked money. He deposited 1,500 dollars of his savings against the finished picture being unreleasable. Sennett was much impressed by this show of self-confidence.

Chaplin soon mastered the primary rules of movie making. They were simple enough in those silent days; all that mattered were entrances and exits. Films followed the stage, actors came on to start a scene, walked, or in Keystone's case, rushed off to end one. There was very little cutting within a scene, although D. W. Griffith, Sennett's mentor, had established the technique some years before. But as the breaking up of a scene into shots required not only careful directing and acting, but also the shooting of extra footage so that action could be overlapped to obtain smooth movement in the cutting, the practise was not encouraged by economy-conscious companies like Keystone. Every foot of film counted as four cents, and to discard exposed film either side of an editor's cut was, to Sennett, throwing dollars in the dustbin. Chaplin was to change all this. Mean with his own money maybe, he would never be mean with a movie. In later years his extravagance with film became Hollywood history; whole reels were exposed for inches used. Meanwhile his generosity with Sennett's celluloid staggered Keystone cameramen and cutters, who put it down to the new director's rawness. The actors, too, suffered from the new director. Used to men like Lehrman who would quickly block out the scene, line them up within their camera limits, and let them pantomime the plot to his shouted instructions, they not only found Chaplin's method unprofessional, indeed amateurish, they found it personally insulting. Seasoned screen performers all, they were embarrassed to have this upstart Englishman, scarcely in the movies a month or more, not only telling them how to act, but showing them too.

'I told the other actors how to play their parts, played them myself to show how it should be done; played my own part enthusiastically, teased the cameramen, laughed and whistled and turned handsprings. The clicking camera took it all in; later, in the negative room, we chose and cut and threw away film, picking out the best scenes, rearranging the reels, shaping up the final picture to be shown on the screen.'[2]

Caught in the Rain was no milestone in movie history or humour. As with his first scenario, Chaplin was content to let his directorial debut follow Keystone tradition. There was the park, the rain, the cheap hotel, and even the arrival spot on schedule of the Keystone Cops. There was also the established figure of Charlie, but this time he had an opponent worthier than half-pint Conklin or slender Kennedy. In charge of his own casting, Chaplin chose mighty Mack Swain: stolid and solid, towering and glowering, fuming over those walrus whiskers he always wore as 'Ambrose'. The comedy contrast of short and tall, slim and stout, had been a Karno cornerstone. Little Chaplin's biggest laughs always came when he bested an outsize opposite. Indeed, David and Goliath was his favourite Bible story, and its theme would pervade his pictures. Charlie and Mack were visual ringers for the legendary opponents, and, more importantly, suited each other's personality both on and off set. Chaplin used Swain whenever he was available, and altogether made twelve films with him in the eight months he had left at Keystone. He was Chaplin's first chum in the picture business, and became founder-member of that select stock company of actors for whom there would always be room in a Chaplin film.

Caught in the Rain also had something else: timing. Time to take for Chaplin to improvize those touches that brought the extra laughs from the audience and the special comments from the critics. Charlie is so drunk he tries to open his door with a cigarette, douses himself with whisky instead of hair-oil, and polishes his shoes with his dickey. There is a surfeit of casual violence and saucy sex. Charlie stomps on an oldster's gouty foot, and Alice Davenport, nightdress a-billow, sleepwalks into his bed. This scene caused quite a stir, less for its explicit sex (you would need to be pretty tipsy to fancy Miss Davenport in or out of her tentlike nightie) than for Charlie's deadpan acceptance of her somnambulent search for his wallet. It was a scene straight from French farce, as was the climax, Charlie in pyjamas locked out in a downpour. But so much plot, packed with tiny gags yet able to take its time when necessary, and all within fifteen minutes of film, was new to the movies.

In the studio viewing theatre it was a full house. 'Every director was present,' wrote Sennett. 'I could hear Dell Henderson, Del Lord and my other comedy makers suck in lungfuls of air, getting ready to let loose jeers and catcalls. Instead, they applauded from the first scene.'[22] Chaplin paced nervously outside. 'I was anxious to know Sennett's

Charlie Squares Up

above : *Making a Living* (1914) with Henry Lehrman

below : *Between Showers* (1914) with Ford Sterling

reaction. I waited for him as he came out of the projection room. "Well, are you ready to start another?" he said.'[1] Chaplin kept his 1,500 dollars.

Chaplin's second film was shot, edited, and shown three days later. He was showing the boss he could move with the best of them when he wanted to, and this time he certainly wanted to: Sennett had promised him a bonus of 25 dollars to bring in a picture within one day! San Pedro was flinging a festival to celebrate the opening of its new harbour. It was the kind of event Lehrman would have leaped at. Chaplin set off with Mack Swain, a cameraman, and some of Alice Davenport's old castoffs. He came back a couple of hours later with a comedy in the can. For the first time in films Charlie appeared as a woman. Not in 'drag', but a full-blown female, Mrs Mack Swain! Drawing on his original success as the camera pest of *Kid Auto Races*, Charlie the virago obstructs the photographer, kicks the director, clobbers the coppers, and ends up being slung into the sea. Chaplin called it *A Busy Day*, which it certainly had been, and Sennett gave him his $25 bonus – and the taste for such extra-contractual delights, as shall be seen.

To set the seal publicly upon their now harmonious partnership, Chaplin, Sennett and Mabel teamed up to make *The Fatal Mallet*. The basic joke, Charlie thumping Sennett and Swain with a monstrous mallet, was old hat when Weber and Fields brought it to vaudeville, but the exaggeration made it funnier than the boot to her bottom that won Mabel's heart. Such rough treatment did not prevent her from appearing in Chaplin's next, which served to introduce Sennett's latest capture and colleague from the Biograph comedies, Charles Murray. Where Ford Sterling specialized in funny Dutchmen, Murray's main line was the funny Frenchman. His characterisation of the Gallic dandy fascinated Chaplin. He not only impersonated Murray in *Her Friend the Bandit*, but carried the character over into many of his later comedies, casting Leo White as the Count again and again. Chaplin's personal observation of the Frenchman in action was not limited to the cinema, although he had always sought out and seen all the Max Linder comedies he could. He had, of course, played in Paris.

Her Friend the Bandit again teamed Mabel and Chaplin as actor/directors. Count De Beans (Murray) is on his way to Mabel De Rock's reception when he is waylaid by Charlie the bandit. Finding the invitation Charlie dons the Count's posh suit and is promptly made welcome by Mabel's mama, eager to overlook his eccentricity on account of his wealth. Mabel, of course, finds Charlie irresistible, but his alcoholic indiscretions are ultimately too much: she calls the cops. It was *Caught in a Cabaret* mixed with *Making a Living*: the monied mama, the eligible beauty, the society reception, and the low posing as the high. It was a good formula and one to which Chaplin would return more than once.

The on-screen kisses Chaplin exchanged with Mabel were now being echoed off. His affair with Peggy Pearce had fizzled and Chaplin was trying again. He put more meaning into these kisses with Mabel, and for a while it seemed that she was responding. But then her spat with Sennett was patched up, and the hoped-for affair failed to fruit. Chaplin had now become an accepted member of the Keystone club, thanks more to his character on screen than off. 'Success makes one endearing', he wrote.[1] Roscoe Arbuckle and his nephew, Al StJohn, lived the Hollywood high life, and took Chaplin along. There were parties and prize fights, and one night Fatty and Charlie climbed into the ring to play comedy seconds to Frank Dolan and Al McNeill. The fun turned into a film when Charles Avery directed Arbuckle in *The Knockout*. Charlie popped up in the 'guest star' role of the referee. It was only two minutes in a two-reeler, but the cries of delighted surprise when the audience saw Charlie come jumping into the ring promoted Chaplin from unbilled bit to co-star billing. Kessel and Baumann in New York advertised *The Knockout* as a Charlie Chaplin picture and reaped an according benefit. Charles Chaplin in Hollywood began to suspect a little of his real worth. Perhaps there would be more than a twelvemonth's work in these flickers after all.

Mabel and Chaplin got together again, but strictly professionally. *Mabel's Busy Day* was a quickie contrived around events at the local auto race track. Charlie is the elegant sharpie shamelessly swiping Mabel's sausages, then playing variations on the *Kid Auto Races* theme with constable George 'Slim' Summerville subbing for director Lehrman. With Charlie brought to repentance by Mabel's charms (and kicks), the two stroll off arm in arm, out of one picture and into the next.

Mabel's Married Life is not an altogether happy one. Husband Charlie sports a topper and cane, but his baggy pants and peeling soles betray their social status. Their lunch is a shared banana on a bench in Westlake Park, yet he has cash to spare when it comes to treating himself to a tot in the café. What plot there is, is nothing but a contrivance for the drunken Charlie to execute a five-minute solo sparring match with a punchbag togged up to look like Mack Swain. From the first few taps to the last wild swings, bouncing both Charlie and Mabel around the room, it is an inspired elaboration of Chaplin's original punchbag encounter in *The Football Match* coupled with his drunken dude from *Mumming Birds*.

There was Karno comedy at the bottom of his next film, too. Dentist sketches had been staple stuff on stage since the *commedia del' arte*, but Chaplin's touches raised *Laughing Gas* above the ruck. Charlie arrives at morning surgery, briskly

Charlie makes a Hit

above : *The Bond* (1918)
with Syd Chaplin

below : *Laughing Gas* (1914)
with Joseph Swickard

greeting his miserable patients, carefully removing hat, cane, and gloves before departing to empty the spittoons. The patients thought such a fine fellow must surely be the dentist; so did the audience. It was a typical Chaplin switch, an opening gag which would quickly become standard yet always a surprise. After silencing an hysterical patient with a handy mallet, and accidentally removing the skirt of the dentist's wife, Charlie takes charge. Carefully selecting the prettiest patient, Chaplin's ill-constructed plot stops to let the camera contemplate Charlie's performance. His improvized examination of the fascinated maiden uses every prop in sight, from swabs to spittoons, from the dental chair that spins and tips to forceps that prove perfect for holding the patient's nose while he kisses her lips. The rest is riot: Slim Summerville and Mack Swain, bleeding at the mouth from brickbats bunged by Charlie, turn up for treatment, and after much kicking in the face and tugging at the teeth, extract their revenge.

That violence breeds violence is a truism borne out by *The Property Man*, the next Chaplin release. Even the trade papers were disturbed: 'There is some brutality in this picture, and we can't help feeling that this is reprehensible. What human being can see an old man kicked in the face and count it as fun?'[29] Chaplin could, of course, or he wouldn't have done it; and it is interesting that in later years, when under the severest criticism, his plea was 'I am nothing more than a human being'. But in 1914 Chaplin was not the only 'French Kicker' in the films. He had received several from Lehrman in that first film, which already seemed long, long ago. Nor was he the funniest. Arbuckle's high kick always brought a laugh, coming so surprisingly from one so plump.

The Property Man is a back-stage *Mumming Birds*, with Charlie behind the scenes as a 'props' instead of in front of them as a drunk. The end result is the same: chaos. Garlico the Strong Man is played by fat Fritz Schade; obviously Chaplin had Mack Swain in mind. Chaplin kicks his ancient assistant into carrying Garlico's trunk of weights, then kicks him some more when he gives way under it. The old gaffer lies pinned beneath the trunk, flailing like an upturned beetle, while Charlie flirts with the Goo-Goo Sisters. Here comes some humour one critic found 'too vulgar to describe'. Charlie hides a glass of beer down the top of his trousers, spills it picking up a Sister's purse, and soaks himself. His subsequent leg-shaking still looks dirty.

The Property Man was the first two-reel (half-hour) film Chaplin had written and directed. It took him three full weeks. This was three times as long as Kessel and Baumann wanted; their exhibitors were calling for a Chaplin a week. Sennett cut Chaplin back to one-reelers. He got what he asked for, but it took longer than a week to make. And small wonder; Chaplin had suddenly abandoned his formula for compromise and

come up with something completely different. In 1914 the dramatic monologue was still a popular art-form. Men in tails or uniform or cowboy costume bestrode the boards between acrobats and double-acts declaiming rhymed epics of Christmas Day in the Workhouse, of dying comrades and dead dogs, and Ladies Known as Lou. They left not a dry eye in the house. One such much-loved ballad was by Hugh Antoine D'Arcy, and from this Chaplin wrought his pace-making burlesque.

In *The Face on the Bar-room Floor* the cinematic vagabond was Charlie, and no summer evening was ever balmier. At Joe's bar-room on the corner of the square he tells his tale, in return for refills, illustrating the subtitled couplets with flashback scenes of his artistic past when he painted a portrait of the nubile Madeleine (the nubile Cecile Arnold). With his own left hand he lovingly limns the outswerving curve of her bustle, but this paradise is lost when rich Fritz Schade makes off with his model. The goodly crowd prompt the end of the story. It is a happy one: when next they meet Madeleine has four brats in tow. Charlie begins to draw the famous Face on the Floor. The goodly crowd kick him out. He starts to chalk it on the sidewalk; a cop kicks him back in. Comes the famous last line: 'With a fearful shriek he leaped and fell across the picture, dead.' To that Charlie adds one word: 'drunk'! It was broad burlesque of the kind Chaplin had worked in *Casey's Circus*, but it was new enough in movies to cause considerable comment, and critics noted Chaplin's differentiation between Charlie 'before and after'.

To catch up on Keystone's release schedule, Sennett sent Chaplin to Westlake Park with a camera and some bricks and told him to make a film in a day. The result was *Recreation* – and another $25 bonus. It was familiar fun: a bench, a girl, a sailor, and a couple of cops with everybody landing in the lake. But it filled in the gap while Chaplin worked on *The Masquerader*. Chaplin plays himself, the film star, and we see him making up as the now famous Tramp. He reports to the set where the director, Charles Murray, eggs on his actors with wild waves of the script (!). Charlie is so distracted by the charms of Cecile Arnold and Vivian Edwards that he misses his cue, and is booted out. Next morning a beautiful young lady draped in white fur and feathers turns up. She flirts with Murray, then cocks a snook behind his back. Off comes the wig and it is Charlie! The kicks-and-bricks finale which drowns Charlie in a well closes a film thick with interest. It catches the flavour of film-making 1914-style, and illumines a new side of Chaplin's talent. Here is no harridan of *A Busy Day*, but a beautiful girl who would fool any fancier.

Chaplin was back in Westlake Park for *His New Profession*, with a plot that had worn out its welcome by 1907. Charlie is hired to push gouty Fritz Schade around in his wheelchair.

Naturally, Charlie's charge ends up in the lake, and as a final indignity is arrested for disturbing the peace! This was the second use of gout as a gag in a Chaplin film, a theme which would be finally and superbly worked out in *The Cure*. His favourite theme, intoxication, was less acceptable in the increasingly middle-class entertainment of the cinema than it was in working-class vaudeville, where Chaplin had perfected it. Even trade critics were frowning on drinking scenes, but when Chaplin and Arbuckle got together for a cinematic hymn to the bottle, *Moving Picture World* reckoned them among the few performers who avoided giving offence in such scenes.[30]

The Rounders are Chaplin (Mr Full) and Arbuckle (Mr Fuller), two top-hatted, evening-caped, gents-about-town who join forces for a jag after trouncings from their wives. Charlie strikes a match on Fritz Schade's bald head, while Fatty rolls himself in a tablecloth, props his feet on a wine bucket, and goes to sleep. The wild wives arrive and, augmented by irate diners, chase the good fellows to a familiar lake. They steal a canoe and lie back to sleep it off, while the crowd roars, the water rises, and the boat sinks. Charlie's floating topper marks his watery grave.

And now, with a string of simple comedies completed, Chaplin took his time, seventeen days of it, to construct with care the prototype photoplay for all his future features. *The New Janitor* is Charlie, of course, but this time he is no 'props' with a helper to harry. He is himself the lowest of the low. Even breezy bellhop Al St John delights in depriving him of the lift, sailing upwards whenever Charlie is summoned aloft from his gloomy basement. Charlie still has his famous flat feet, but this time they are souvenirs of his weary years, and obviously hurt as he humps mop and pail up flight after flight to answer the strident bell. Minta Durfee, pretty and efficient, loves Jack Dillon, clerk: an emotion beautifully and economically conveyed by her glance at his straw hat on the office coat-rack. Charlie, washing a window, almost falls out; his bucket falls, of course, on President Fritz Schade. Charlie is sacked, letting Chaplin the director get to work. He lets us forget Charlie and comedy for a surprising time while Jack is threatened with exposure for a gambling debt, robs the safe, and is discovered by Minta. They fight, and in the struggle Jack forces Minta against the porter's button. In the basement the bell rings, but why should Charlie answer it? He has been sacked, he is ready to go home, it's a long way to the top floor, and his feet hurt. Chaplin pulls out the suspense like a Griffith. Charlie starts the long climb and liftboy Al does his vanishing trick. He turns to go back – Minta swoons – he changes his mind, but the climb is so hard on his feet that he almost fails to make the top floor. But one sight of the crime and Charlie swings into action, whacking Jack with his cane, whipping up the dropped gun and covering the crook from between his legs, shooting

out of the window to attract attention. A cop arrives, takes one look at Charlie, and arrests him. It is the first Chaplin comment on the stigma of class marked by clothing. Luckily Minta unswoons in time to save him, and President Schade presents him with a wad of notes – which Charlie is quick to count before thanking him.

All this and more, much more, has taken but one thousand and twenty feet of film to tell. It shows Chaplin as master of the dramatic as well as the comic: compare the pantomime of Minta Durfee, so broad in *The Rounders*, so natural in *The New Janitor*. It shows Chaplin's control over both actor and editor. Above all it shows Chaplin as a maturing performer: his basic Charlie has a new dimension. No longer 'quaint' or 'whimsical', the favourite critical terms, he is human, a lifetime of drudgery bending his back, years of stair-climbing weighting his feet. Alice Davenport, watching on the sidelines, wiped an eye as Charlie, pleading to Schade for his job, pantomimed a large family of assorted offspring. 'I know its supposed to be funny', she said, 'but you just make me weep.' Wrote Chaplin, 'She confirmed something I already felt: I had the ability to evoke tears as well as laughter.'[1]

Chaplin's next film was simple stuff. *Those Love Pangs* teamed Charlie and Chester with as saucy a pair of flirts as ever winked and beckoned from a pre-permissive screen – Cecile Arnold and Vivian Edwards. Chaplin had begun the film with a scene establishing Charlie and Chester as rivals in a bakery. So much fun came from it that he decided to cut it out of the picture and expand it into a full film. Sennett budgeted it at a thousand dollars, top whack for a two-reeler. Chaplin brought it in at 800 over. There was no bonus this time, but for Sennett there was. *Dough and Dynamite* took over $130,000 in its first year of release, and even more when Sennett reissued it in 1923 with funny new subtitles written by Syd Chaplin.

Dough and Dynamite, claimed a critic, 'is one of the cleanest that Keystone has done'.[31] Perhaps he missed the subtle sign beside those pretty waitresses, Mam'zelles Arnold and Edwards: 'Assorted French Tarts'. The bakers in the employ of Monsieur Fritz Schade go on strike, so the waiters, Charlie and Chester, are put in charge of the kitchen. The waitresses, who smile impartially on either and sit nonchalantly in pastry, stir the rivalry and soon flour is flying in the kitchen. The strikers stick dynamite in a loaf, and as unsatisfied customers, irate proprietors, and berserk waiters join in floury battle, the dynamite explodes. Matters reach a head: rising from the swelling dough comes Charlie's unsinkable face.

Chester Conklin, who had now joined the lifetime society of Chaplin regulars, teamed with Charlie again as the *Gentlemen of Nerve*. In this one-day quickie improvized around a familiar race track, Charlie is identified as 'Mr Wow-Wow' in an echo of Karno days.

By this time the good burghers of Hollywood and environs were beginning to resent the haywire intrusions of the movie men into their working world. It was not so bad when they mucked about at the auto races, but when Chaplin and chums arrived with a donkey cart to shoot sequences for *His Musical Career* outside the Song Shop on Spring Street, traffic was blocked for hours. Only Charlie's fame saved him from arrest. The film casts him as a workman again: you can tell by his clay pipe. Charlie and mighty Mack must deliver a new piano to Mr Rich of 666 Prospect Street, and remove an old piano from Mr Poor of 999. Naturally they get their missions mixed. There is a hill for the piano and Charlie to run down, and a river for them to land in. Charlie adds his individual touch to this familiar finale: he plays a final requiem before the piano carries him under. But the deeps cannot hold him, any more than they could in *The Rounders*. Charlie was back on the screen but two days later, in another two-reel special.

His Trysting Place presents a picture of the home life of Charlie and Mabel, and it is one which must have been all too familiar to his working-class audience. The delights of saucy courtship, so often depicted in past pictures, have tarnished into domestic drudgery. Wifey tries to make bread and tend baby at the same time and on the same table, while hubby tries to relax with his feet up – and tips over a boiling kettle. It is all quite a contrast to the home life of Mr and Mrs Swain: love and kisses in an opulent apartment. The opposing ends of the social scale collide at the counter of a café. Mack sups soup and Charlie gnaws a bone. The poor man, so fastidious that he wipes his fingers on an old man's beard, is repulsed by the rich man's manners. A duel begins, rising from a flick of gravy to the full French kick. Charlie scoots away, taking Mack's coat by mistake. Mabel finds a billet-doux in the pocket and bends the ironing board over Charlie's head. But there is worse in store for Mack: his wife looks in his pocket and finds a baby bottle! Chaplin based his comedy of errors on an old comic song his father had sung in vaudeville; but the human quality he added was all his own.

While Chaplin had been churning out his one and two reelers, Sennett had been labouring long over a personal ambition, to produce the first feature-length comedy in film history. As far back as April 1914 he had signed Marie Dressler, the famous stage comedienne, for a film version of her big success, *Tillie's Nightmare*. Personality problems and script problems dragged the production into July, then Kessel and Baumann were too nervous to release it. Marie Dressler sued to gain control of the film, Justice Newburger dismissed her claim, and Kessel and Baumann sold it outright to the independent Alco Corporation for a hundred thousand dollars. As *Tillie's Punctured Romance* it has been in release ever since, on various gauges, at various lengths, and with various soundtracks.

Charlie in Skirts

above: *A Woman* (1915)

below: *A Busy Day* (1914)

inset: *The Masquerader* (1914)

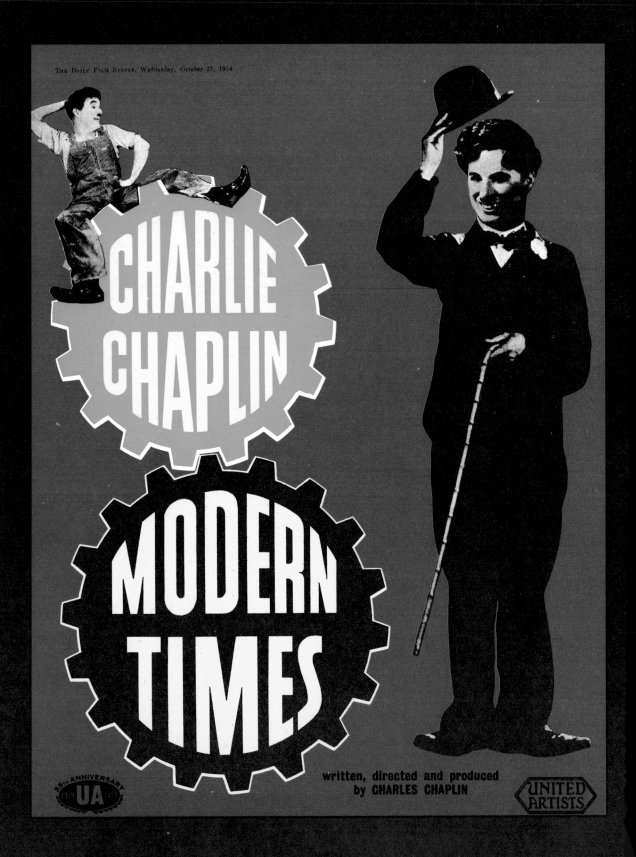

CHARLIE CHAPLIN

MODERN TIMES

35TH ANNIVERSARY
UA
1919 1954

written, directed and produced
by CHARLES CHAPLIN

UNITED ARTISTS

The Rounders (1914) with
Roscoe Arbuckle

If Edgar Smith's original play had been a burlesque, then Hampton Del Ruth's scenario burlesqued the burlesque. The corny old story of city slicker luring pretty country heiress astray became wild enough through the casting of Chaplin and Dressler, but with Sennett directing, wildness was too mild a word. It was a 6,000 foot anthology of all he held dear. Small wonder one critic called it 'the *Cabiria* of comedy'.

Chaplin, billed second above Mabel, is back as the heartless sharper. Perhaps deliberately, certainly fortunately, he wears clothes and whiskers far removed from Charlie's. As to his style, his few short months in movies showed one lesson which Miss Dressler, in her screen debut, had failed to learn. Chaplin neither mugs nor semaphores his emotions. Marie would learn, of course, and in time become the talkie's greatest character star, but in November 1914 her ugly grimaces and over-done makeup are even more grotesque against the controlled Chaplin. Indeed, Chaplin is so nonchalant, so deadpan, that the young Buster Keaton might have found inspiration here. 'Chaplin's serious face is seldom crossed by a smile. With perfect confidence he leaves laughter to others; and well he may.'[32]

In later years, Chaplin would survey the huge crew and impedimenta of modern movie making and sigh for the old times when 'All I needed to make a picture was a park, a policeman, and a pretty girl'. One morning in November 1914 he went down to Westlake with Mabel, Mack Swain, and Edgar Kennedy bearded like a Turk. He came back with *Getting Acquainted*, his best and last Keystone quickie and his last bonus from Sennett. Its action is indescribable, more choreographed than scripted, as the actors untangle their complex affairs with a good deal of beating around the bush.

It was time to make his last Keystone Comedy, his 35th film in 52 weeks. *His Prehistoric Past* is a burlesque, taking as its butt the contemporary craze for prehistoric pictures that Griffith had initiated with *Man's Genesis*. The great director had called his hero Weakhands; Chaplin calls himself Weakchin. But so familiar is the bearskinned figure that flatfoots over the mountain complete with derby and cane that we hail him as Charlie. When he flirts with the grass-skirted maidens of the cave community he does so with his back to the camera, flapping his tail in lieu of coat-tails in a reprise of the back-view courtship he introduced to movies in *Between Showers*. Charlie deposes King Lowbrow (Mack Swain) with a kick over the cliff, but pansy Fritz Schade saves him with a handy snake. Lowbrow breaks a boulder over Charlie's head and he wakes to find himself on a familiar park bench, a cop thumping him with a truncheon. It was all a dream, a plot twist dating back to *Jimmy the Fearless* and one which would become a favourite in the future.

Poster for *Modern Times*

Charlie is ordered to move on; and Chaplin moved on, too.

5
A Film Johnnie
(1915-1916)

THE KEYSTONE FILM CO.

The Tramp (1915) with
Paddy McGuire

Essanay Announces It Has Secured
CHARLES CHAPLIN
The Greatest Comedian the motion picture world
has ever seen. This inimitable laugh-maker is
at work now on some Essanay comedies that will
be released in the near future. You know what
Charles Chaplin means to your box office!

The full page advertisement in *Moving Picture World* dated January 2, 1915, confirmed the sensational news of the previous week: 'Essanay signs Charles Chaplin! The announcement was made in New York on Monday evening, 14 December 1914, by George K. Spoor, president of the Essanay Film Manufacturing Company, that Charles Chaplin, famous screen comedian, had signed with his company. The information was contained in a telegram from G. M. Anderson from Niles, California.'[33] Gilbert Anderson, ex Max Aaronson, was better known in the business as 'Broncho Billy'. He had been the world's first cowboy star; now he was the 'Ay' to George K. Spoor's 'Ess' in the Chicago-based company of 'Essanay'. In all his hundreds of weekly westerns, Broncho had never roped a bigger winner.

Chaplin's contract with Keystone was due to expire in December. Two months earlier, Sennett started casting around for a new comedian. Chaplin recommended his brother, and on October 31st, Syd and Charlie were reunited. Syd signed with Sennett for 200 dollars a week, twenty-five more than Chaplin was getting: Charlie considered his old debts well paid. Syd was full of the great business Chaplin films were doing at home in England, and, taking charge of his junior as in days of old, urged him to demand a rise. So when Sennett called him into the office to discuss a new contract, Chaplin asked for a thousand dollars a week. Sennett was thunderstruck: 'But *I* don't make that!', he said. Chaplin pointed out it was not Sennett's name that drew the crowds. Sennett agreed to try it on Kessel and Baumann. They wired back an offer, to rise from $500 to $1000 over three years. But Chaplin, unable to see his popularity, or indeed creativity, lasting beyond another twelvemonth, stuck to his demand. Sennett turned him down flat. As his last two months slipped by, Chaplin began to worry. Jesse J. Robbins arrived in town.

Over dinner at the Los Angeles Athletic Club, where Chaplin roomed at twelve dollars a week, Robbins laid out his offer. Essanay had authorized him to propose $1250 a week, but he was not sure about the bonus. Bonus, queried Chaplin, king of the dead pan. Yes, Mr Robbins understood that Mr Chaplin required $10,000 cash before signing a contract. Mr Robbins understood correctly, said Mr Chaplin. Mr Robbins then telephoned Mr Anderson, and the deal was on! Chaplin shook hands with Sennett, kissed Mabel, bid yet another family farewell to Syd and his wife, and took the train to Chicago.

He clocked in at 1333 Argyle Street on 2 January, 1915. Immediately there was trouble. Spoor was nowhere to be found, so neither was Chaplin's money. The scenario editor, a Miss Louella Parsons, handed him a script, and was most surprised to be told the new star wrote his own. He was given a director, who was equally surprised to learn the star directed himself. He was given the pick of the casting office, which meant any actor on stock who was currently unemployed. Chaplin recognized only one of the remnant group, a comic whose crossed eyes had been making audiences laugh for a decade. In Ben Turpin Chaplin picked a worthy adversary. He led his selected crowd to the studio. What scenery did he require, what props would he want, where did he want the camera placed? And what on earth was he going to do? There wasn't an idea in his head, and the efficient Essanay organization was geared to a shooting-script system. Not for nothing did they advertize themselves as 'The first to standardize photoplays'. Chaplin looked around him and the idea came. He would use the studio itself as his set, the objects that surrounded him as his props, the situation he found himself in as his plot. He called it *His New Job*.

Chaplin took a good-humoured swipe at his old employer by opening with Charlie's arrival at the Lockstone Studio, looking for work. After a brisk battle with Ben and a swift squirt of ink down the manager's deaf-aid, he stands in for an extra on the set of *A King's Ransom*. He makes an hilarious hussar in a shaggy shako: Chaplin's first use in films of exaggerated costume. At the height of the drama he kneels at the feet of Charlotte Mineau. Spurning his ardour she ascends the stairs, unconscious of the fact that her skirt is trapped beneath his knees. Charlie blows his nose on the torn train: a signal for an all stops out finale involving punches and hammerings, kicks and ink. Said Chaplin, 'It is the very best comedy I have ever produced. The new surroundings and clever actors whom I had to work with enabled me to make the greatest comedy of my life. I couldn't help laughing when I saw it on the screen.'[34]

But behind the screen Chaplin was less happy than his public face showed in the publicity photographs which lined him up with G. M. Anderson and Francis X. Bushman as 'Essanay's A.B.C. of Stars'. Spoor did not turn up at the studio until after the film was finished. Chaplin was quick to confront him. Spoor had privately considered that his partner had gone mad, and only the arrival of an unprecedented number of advance orders for Chaplin's first Essanay release reconciled him to Chaplin's equally unprecedented salary. Spoor paid up, but still Chaplin was unhappy. Even the hectic atmosphere of Keystone was more conducive to his style of moviemaking than the highly organized production-line of Essanay. He needed time to await inspiration, time to improvise, and silence for concentration. Spoor suggested he try the

Behind the Screen (1916) with Mabel Normand and Eric Campbell

overleaf: Charlie's best
Friend

The Gold Rush (1925)

company's California studio where Anderson made his Broncho Billys.

Chaplin went west and took Ben Turpin with him. He also took Rolland H. Totheroh, the staff cameraman who had made such a good job of *His New Job*. Chaplin's film technique was as basic as could be, but he had learned from E. J. Vallejo the Keystone cameraman that the framing of each shot was the key to cinema. 'I found that the placing of the camera was not only psychological, but articulated a scene; in fact, it was the basis of cinematic style. If the camera is a little too near, or too far, it can enhance or spoil an effect. Placement of camera is cinematic inflection.'[1] Totheroh was as competent a picture-framer as any cameraman of the period, and could use the incoming techniques when required. There is one 'trucking shot' in *His New Job*, but it is used quietly and to Chaplin's credo. The camera approaches the set of *A King's Ransom*, gradually cutting out the studio personnel until the actors fill the screen. Chaplin was well pleased with the effect, but neither man could know it would be the start of a forty year association. Chaplin called Totheroh 'Rollie', yet forgot to mention him in his 545-page autobiography.

Before training back to warm California, Chaplin gave his first ever interviews. Nothing excites the press more than money, and 'The Highest Salaried Comedian in the World' was a natural headline. E. V. Whitcomb interviewed him for *Photoplay* and found 'the funniest thing about this extremely funny man is his violet-like reluctance to talk about Charlie Chaplin. "There is nothing worth talking about", he says. "I am no one – just a plain fellow. There is absolutely nothing interesting about me."'[35] Chaplin, whom Whitcomb described as 'a very lovable lad, with a delicate sensitive face and with his hair painstakingly wetted and smoothed down', could hardly have realized that he would become the most written-about celebrity in cinema history.

Chaplin was totally unprepared for the press to probe into his private life. These early biographies are full of falsehoods: 'I have never had a day's schooling in my life; my mother taught us what she could, but after she died, I was an apprentice to a company of travelling acrobats, jugglers, and show-people. I came to New York with my brother Sidney while I was still a boy.'[35] Five months later he was claiming to have been born in Fontainebleau during a continental tour of his parent's company.[36] The facts were as fictional as the Charlie Chaplin strips that began to appear in the comics, first in England by Bertie Brown, then in America by Elzie Segar. The Chaplin Industry was under way, and as Charlie's face beamed from newspaper and magazine, song-sheet and toy shop, so too the knocking began.

'Billie Ritchie, in order to settle, allay, and to put the quietus on all controvertionalists who contest his claims to having

originated the "drunk" make-up he now uses in those screaming L-KO Comedies (produced incidentally by Henry
Lehrman) wishes to announce that he first used his present
make-up in 1887, three years before Charles Chaplin was
born. How's that for a left-handed slam?'[37] Ritchie claimed he
created the Tramp's make-up and costume for *Early Birds* and
Chaplin's drunk act for *Mumming Birds*; three months later
Sigmund Lubin claimed the same thing on behalf of his new
star, Billy Reeves. Chaplin, of course, owed much to both
Billies, but as they soon discovered, there was more to Charlie
than mere makeup.

Chaplin installed himself at Anderson's outpost in Niles. If
his first for Essanay had clear Keystone connections, so had
his second. *His Night Out*, which became *One Night Out*, and
finally *A Night Out*, was devoted to the slapstick staggers of
a couple of drunks, Turpin replacing that old Rounder,
Arbuckle. The set builders struggled with the required café
interior: western saloons were more in their line. While they
were getting it to suit Chaplin he went down to San Francisco
in search of a girl. One of Broncho Billy's cowboys recommended a pretty miss who frequented Tate's Café on Hill
Street. Thus Edna Purviance, a nineteen year old unemployed
stenographer from Paradise Valley, Nevada, beautiful and
comfortably covered, refreshingly untutored in the arts of
Thespis, became Trilby to Chaplin's Svengali. Edna was
everything Chaplin needed, in an actress and in a woman.
Putty in his creative hands, she followed his instructions
implicitly, echoing his every suggested gesture. And as
Charlie's character evolved, deepened, became richer, so did
Edna's. Their harmony was so obvious the world longed for
them to make it come true off-screen as well as on. Chaplin
longed for it, too, but his heart broke again when he discovered
she preferred Thomas Meighan. But she went on to partner
Chaplin in virtually every film he made during the next
decade, and remained on his payroll until she died, on the
thirteenth of January, 1958.

Edna's first on-screen encounter with Charlie was a saucy
one. Stooping to unlock her door in *A Night Out* she narrowly
misses having drunk Charlie squat on her bottom. He squints
through her keyhole and what he sees makes him grab a
syphon from a passing bellboy, squirt seltzer down his
trousers, then lift one leg to let the liquid run out! While he
is in his bathroom, the night-attired Edna enters his bedroom
in search of her dog. Charlie is delighted to find Edna
under his bed. Sneaking her back to her room, her husband's
arrival forces Charlie to hide in her bed. Charlie is sat upon,
exposed, and shot at. He ends up in the bath, spouting like a
fountain, until once again the waters of fate close over him.

By *The Rounders* out of *Mabel's Strange Predicament*, this
fast farce was nevertheless full of impromptu gags. One

brilliant inspiration was the casting of giant Bud Jamison as Edna's husband. Chaplin had spotted this 21-year old pianist entertaining the customers in a San Francisco café. He found Bud funny and took him to Niles as a kind of court jester. He was useful for accompanying Chaplin's violin, an old pastime to which the comedian was increasingly turning in the long, lonely hours of the Niles night. *A Night Out*, for a movie début, was superb, and Jamison found a life-long career as a Hollywood 'heavy'.

Chaplin's next film marks the first time he came into conflict with the forces of religion. A New Jersey exhibitor played *The Champion* with *The Passion Play* on Good Friday. Even *Moving Picture World* was shocked: 'A Chaplin farce billed above *The Passion Play* is so far beyond the limit that it is out of sight. That's the sort of thing that arouses the antagonism of church people and helps along censorship moves.'[38] *The Champion* is a reworking of *The Knockout* with Chaplin in the Arbuckle role. Burlesque boxing was regular Karno comedy, but it is Chaplin's trimmings that count. Charlie is given a new dimension by a bulldog, who shares both his trampings and his frankfurter. One of Charlie's first touches of humanity; it is typical that the human outcast should find it with a dog. Yet there is a joke to this love, too. Hungry Charlie won't eat until his dog has first bite, and the dog won't eat until he gets salt on the sausage! Sparring partners are required by Lloyd Bacon, champ. Charlie finds a horseshoe, stuffs it up his glove for luck, and lays Lloyd low. As the new contender Charlie gets a chance to rework all those Karno stunts with Indian clubs, punchbags and barbells. He shows off to Edna, a cuddly sport in sweater and cap, and does his back-to-camera flirtation bit. Count Leo White tempts him to throw the fight, but Charlie's dog bounds into the ring, hanging grimly from the champion's shorts until Charlie delivers the knockout blow. A few weeks later Spike the bull-dog was killed by a car. He holds an honoured place in movie memory as the little fellow's first dog.

Essanay hoped for a film a fortnight from Chaplin, and at first he tried to maintain this schedule. To balance out the time-taking two-reelers he resorted to Keystone ways and churned out a typical quickie with a typical title, *In The Park*. Charlie wanders through the Niles version of Westlake, kicks Count Leo into the pond, and makes away with the nursemaid Edna.

Romance first touched Charlie's soul in *A Jitney Elopement*. Here his love for Edna is pure. There are no pats on bottoms, sticks up skirts, or sudden bursts of lust. Instead there is the hopeless love of poor for rich, soulfully expressed as he toys with a daffodil and casts cow-eyes at her balcony. To oblige her he poses as Count Leo White, whom her father (Fred Goodwins) requires her to marry. Charlie's supposed

Charlie takes the Road

The Tramp (1915)

wealth excuses his every eccentricity: at dinner he sprinkles salt on a flower and eats it, peels a roll like an orange, blows his nose on the tablecloth, and drinks hot coffee until steam spouts from his ears. The action-packed car chase involving the real Count and the cops is excellently engineered, considering it was the kind of Keystone climax that Chaplin claimed to despise.

While he was in San Francisco, Chaplin met a tramp. He offered him food and drink, and asked him which he would like first. 'Why', said the hobo, 'If I am hungry enough, I can eat grass. But what am I going to do for this thirst of mine? You know what water does to iron? Well, try to think what it will do for your insides!' Chaplin took him to a bar and listened in fascination to the joys and hardships of hobo life. 'He was rather surprised when we parted, because I thanked him so much. But he had given me a good deal more than I had given him.'[39] He had given Chaplin not just the title and plot of his next film, but the inspiration to deepen both the character of Charlie and the quality of Chaplin's moviemaking. Chaplin sat down and wrote a rounded-out story; spent time with Totheroh choosing locations and selecting set-ups; acted out each part with his players, rehearsing each scene again and again. And three weeks later came up with the first true Chaplin classic.

The Tramp comes flat-footing down a country road, a familiar if dusty figure. The derby, the cane, the worn boots, and one thing more, his little bundle of worldly goods. It marks him instantly as a human being as real as the road he walks. Then the laughs start: a car roars round the bend bowling him over, instantly followed by another from the opposite direction. Fastidious as ever, Charlie produces a feather duster and dusts himself down, then dines on a handful of grass, made palatable by a dash of salt – his grimaces a tribute to the tramp who inspired the scene. Farmer Fred Goodwins digs deep in his sock to provide daughter Edna with market money, but as she heads for town, Leo White leaps on her. Charlie dashes to the rescue, but then fights a much harder battle – with himself. His good side wins and he hands back Edna's cash. She takes him home to meet dad, who says if Charlie wants a meal he must work for it. He tries milking the cow by pumping her tail, and while gathering eggs, pops one in his pocket, gets it broken during a brief snuggle with Edna, and shuffles off to a flowerbed where he raises a leg and shakes it. That night Leo and his pals burgle the farm; while Charlie is chasing them away the farmer opens fire and hits Charlie in the leg. As Edna bathes his forehead Charlie faints. Fade in on the invalid taking his ease under Edna's sweet care. Then her beau comes calling. His love dream shattered, Charlie goes brokenly into the house to write a note of farewell. He turns away to hide his tears. By using the simple yet brilliant theatrical device of

Charlie on the Fiddle

left : *Limelight* (1952)

above : *Limelight* (1952)
with Snub Pollard

below : in the recording
studio

playing with his back to the audience, Chaplin increases the heartbreak of this scene a thousandfold. Charlie shuffles back down that country road, returning to wherever he came from, weighed down with more than his bundle. Suddenly he shakes off the sadness, squares his shoulders, kicks up his heels, and flip-flaps into the horizon. For the first time, the classic Chaplin fadeout.

The Tramp was the last film Chaplin made at Niles. Although he found the facilities primitive and the backwoods life depressing, without them *The Tramp* might never have been made; the absolute authenticity of its country lanes and farmyard add immeasurably to its atmosphere. From 8 April 1915 the Chaplin company occupied the converted Bradbury Mansion at 147 North Hill Street, Los Angeles. Jesse Robbins was still in charge as 'general producing manager', with Ernest Van Pelt as Chaplin's assistant, Harry Ensign as chief photographer, Fritz Wintermeier manager, and M. A. Brislauer the 'exploitation expert'. Brislauer got going first, getting Chaplin to lead the Venice Tigers parade to mark the opening of the baseball season. He also had him pose for press pictures with 'great people, mayors, actresses, and everything imaginable, even being snapped with animals and an automobile'.[40] Chaplin was news.

While the new studio was being readied, Chaplin filled in with a quickie improvised around Crystal Pier. *By the Sea* introduced to movies another Chaplin 'china' from Karno's army, Billy Armstrong. Together they fight a dandified Jamison with ice cream. Old stuff, but not as old as the opening gag: Charlie eats a banana and slips on the skin!

On the first of May a Mr I. Presburg, manager of the Arena Amusement Company of New York, called George K. Spoor in Chicago. Would Charles Chaplin personally appear to open his new picture show at Madison Square Garden, and play a two-week engagement? Mr Presburg would pay Mr Chaplin $25,000 for the privilege. Spoor said no; Essanay releases must be maintained. Presburg leaked the news to the *Los Angeles Examiner*, who called Chaplin. He promptly called Anderson. Anderson stalled. On May 10 Spoor took the midnight express, meeting Anderson in Oakland on May 13. Chaplin had decided Essanay could not prevent a stage engagement, provided he delivered his contracted films. On May 14 Anderson drew a cheque for $25,000 on the Fort Dearborn National Bank of Chicago, and handed it to Chaplin. 'He gets the Twenty-Five Thousand Dollars Just the Same' was the headline, 'The transaction is probably without precedent in amusement history'.[40] Two weeks later the Arena Amusement Co. went bankrupt. 'Such was my luck', wrote Chaplin.

More luck: on his way to the studio from the Stoll Hotel, where he roomed, Chaplin saw a painter pushing a two-wheeled barrow up the hill. The weight of the paint was too much for the man, and it suddenly tipped him up, over the lot, which spilled into the road. Everybody laughed, and so did Chaplin. It became the opening scene of his next film. *Work* begins with Charlie pulling the two-wheeled cart, but like a work-horse, whipped by his brutal boss. The hill is a full 45 degrees, exaggerated by Rollie's skilful camera placement and Charlie's slipping and sliding. They arrive at a fine house furnished in the latest taste: a naked lady supports a lampshade. Charlie is instantly obsessed. He turns the lampshade into a skirt and makes it hula-hula. And once the naked lady is covered, of course Charlie must peep under her skirt. ('The Censor Board is passing matter in the Chaplin films that could not possibly get by in other pictures', said *Variety*.) After predictable slapstick rooted in *Repairs* and other music hall mainstays, Edna finds Charlie in her bedroom, rolled in sticky wallpaper. They sit on the bed and Charlie mimes to Edna the story of his life. It develops into the expected flirtation, and the dandlings of his pastebrush take on new meaning. ('It is disgusting at many points', *Variety*). Although Chaplin would return to his much-loved mess, notably in *The Circus* and *A King in New York*, the core of the comedy is the mime in the middle, a pure piece of pantomime pointing the way to *The Pilgrim*.

Chaplin hurt his elbow making *Work*, and apologized for it to the Photoplayers Club, which had assembled to be entertained by him on the night of May 13th. Henry B. Walthall announced that Charlie would lead the orchestra. Arbuckle and co. roared with expectant laughter, but it quickly died as Chaplin took the band through Sousa's *Stars and Stripes Forever*. It was the first inkling the public had that Chaplin was a musician. Brislauer told the papers. Within weeks Chaplin had composed three songs and set up his own music publishing company. Elsie Codd, an English lady he had taken on as secretary-cum-publicist, described one of them: 'He tells us a sad little story of lost love with a most haunting refrain.'[41]

> 'There's always one you can't forget,
> There's always one, one vain regret;
> Tho' grief is dead, mem'ry survives,
> Fate linked, we two mated our lives.
> Why did we meet, only to part?
> Love comes but once into the heart;
> Tho' it may cause pain and regret,
> There's always one you can't forget.'

Elsie suspected he sang of Edna, but the old Karno 'plonks' knew better. Chaplin sang of Hetty Kelly, 'a brown-eyed gazelle' who had danced with Bert Coutts' Yankee Doodle Girls, and whom he had loved and lost as a lad of nineteen. Although no photograph of pretty Hetty has come down to us, we can suspect that her image has, through Lita Grey, Paulette Goddard, and especially Oona O'Neill.

right: *A Night in the Show* (1915)

below: *The Bank* (1915) adapted for a boys' story paper, cover by Philip Swinnerton

Still uncomfortable, Chaplin demanded another studio. Robbins found the Rolfe, ex-Majestic, at 651 Fairview Avenue in Boyle Heights. Bigger and better (the stage was 125 feet by 60), it was here that Chaplin first instituted that strict security that would so upset those who could not appreciate his need for uninterrupted concentration. 'A lock has been put on a big new door, and no one can enter the studio where Charlie Chaplin is at work. We had to use a pass key, a shelaleh, and a stick of dynamite to get into the sanctum sanctorum of the great Pooh Bah this week.'[42]

Chaplin was shooting *A Woman*, a revamp of another Keystone theme, female impersonation. Again the female characterisation was perfect, the comedy hilarious, but the reasons for everything contrived and slight. *Variety* pinpointed the weakness: 'Chaplin needs a scenario writer very, very badly.' Perhaps Chaplin took note, for after his next film *Variety* was able to say 'Chaplin must have followed some sort of book in making this film.' In fact, so much writing and rehearsal went into *The Bank* that it was a week late for its release date.

The Bank opens with one of Chaplin's best scene-setters: Charlie arrives with dignity, consults his cuffs for the combination, swings open the safe, and takes out a mop and pail! Yes, he is only the janitor, once again. The plot gets under way with a note from Edna. She has a tie for the cashier's birthday and types 'To Charlie with love'. The janitor, who bears the same name, thinks Edna means him. But his happy heart

67

breaks when he sees Edna tear up his reply and tip his stolen bouquet into her waste-basket. He dozes off. Crooks now hold up Edna and the cashier. Charlie, aroused by Edna's scream, springs into action, laying the thieves low with both sacks and kicks. The cowardly cashier is sacked, and Edna goes to Charlie. Charlie strokes her hair, and the scene dissolves. Charlie is caressing his mop. It was all a dream. The final blow: he sees Edna kissing her Charlie. Our Charlie disposes of the flowers with a typical back-kick. Love is a dream and not for him.

Syd Chaplin, doing well at Keystone, now did even better for his brother. He suggested to Anderson a new way of marketing Charlie's comedies. If rentals were scaled to seating capacity, receipts could be doubled. Essanay tried it and it worked. Naturally, Chaplin wanted a cut. In July Spoor took the train again and gave Chaplin a $10,000 bonus, with the promise of another for every film left on their contract.

As a film-maker, Chaplin had learned his trade at Keystone. His rule was exteriors are shot on location, interiors are shot in the studio. Thus, having written a burlesque maritime melodrama, Chaplin must needs go to sea to shoot it. Hiring a ship was not enough; he had Essanay buy a 200-foot steam schooner, the S.S. *Vaquero*. So his climax could come as a genuine thrill – he blew it to pieces outside Los Angeles harbour. But first came an unscripted thrill. Bad weather marooned the entire company of eighteen off the Californian coast. Jesse Robbins rowed for the shore in the skiff and was almost drowned when it capsized. Chaplin himself semaphored a distress signal to the Venice wireless station, and at last rescue came.

'We must destroy the boat as we need the insurance money.' The concise opening subtitle sets the plot of *Shanghaied*; the rest is laughter. The mate promises Charlie a buck for every sailor he shanghais. Hiding in a barrel with a Keystone mallet he thumps three, thumps the Captain, and is thumped himself. The sea rises, the ship pitches, and Charlie does his unlevel best to get a pile of plates across the tipsy deck to the Captain's cabin. But when he comes to eat his own lunch he sits next to one of those foul-mouthed munchers who put Charlie off at the steadiest of times. When this hungry tar douses his fat pork with lamp-oil, Charlie's gorge rises. He flops down a hatchway and sees a ghost: stowaway Edna in a flour sack!

In his first 'thrill comedy', Chaplin cross-cuts between the lighted dynamite and the owner racing to stop the scuttling. It was a way to build suspense that Griffith had originated and now perfected in *The Birth of a Nation*. This milestone in American movie making had opened at Clune's Los Angeles Auditorium on 8 February 1915. Everybody went, Chaplin more than once. To him it became a university course in the art and craft of cinema. *Shanghaied* also shows interesting use of the camera itself. Totheroh and Ensign devised a counter-

Charlie and the Cops

left: *Police* (1916)

above: *Easy Street* (1917)

below: *Getting Acquainted* (1914)

weight to swing the camera and suggest the ship's tips. Unfortunately nobody realized that this would also tilt the horizon!

A Night in the Show mixed the old and the new. Basing his story on *Mumming Birds* Chaplin recreated his tipsy swell ('Mr Pest') and, wearing walrus whiskers and his old clay pipe, also played a lowlife loudmouth, (Mr Rowdy). Thus he could cause chaos in auditorium and on stage on two levels: the upper class drunk in the stalls and the lower class lout in the gallery. A fire-hose proved extremely useful.

In October 1915 the Jesse Lasky Feature Film Company put forth the De Mille brothers' adaptation of Prosper Merimée's *Carmen*. In November William Fox presented Raoul Walsh's version. In December Essanay announced Chaplin's. And they continued to announce it week by week until April 1916, when at long last *Charlie Chaplin's Burlesque on 'Carmen'* was released. By then, Chaplin had left Essanay and the film had grown from two reels to four. Public demand to see this 'first Chaplin feature' was incredible: 'Crowds not only Break all Box-Office Records but Entrance Doors as Well!' was the headline to the report from Leon D. Langsfield, manager of the Broadway Theatre, New York. 'The heavy copper doors were simply torn off their hinges by the rushing, pushing crowds.'[43] But a perceptive critic considered *Carmen* would be vastly stronger in two reels instead of four: 'In the fight near the close one situation is plainly duplicated, the inference being that the stunt was done twice, that the better of the two might be chosen.'[44] Chaplin agreed – so wholeheartedly that he sued. In the New York Supreme Court he sought an injunction against the distribution of *Carmen*, alleging that the expansion of his two-reeler into four violated his rights as actor, author and producer, and injured his reputation. Essanay counter-sued for breach of contract and damages. On May 24, Judge Hotchkiss dismissed Chaplin's claim on five points, the second of which was crucial: 'The play itself is undoubtedly the property of Essanay, by which company plaintiff was employed.'[45] As Spoor put it, 'We have paid Chaplin for 16,000 feet of negative made taking *Carmen*, and our contract gives us the right to use any or part of anything he made for us.'[46] Chaplin appealed, but lost again.

Charlie Chaplin's Burlesque on 'Carmen': few films can have had a more honest title. It is Casey Court travesty, right down to two men in a pantomime horse skin. The clash between this kind of theatrical comedy and the realism of the setting – Chaplin shot the film at the Santa Monica seashore – is quite unacceptable, and would have made the film a poor one even without the padding. The early scenes feature boss-eyed Ben Turpin and the kind of punning subtitles which were just coming in. Both were added after Chaplin's departure. Charlie plays Don José, punned into Darn Hosiery; Edna puffs a saucy cigarette as a comely Carmen. Charlie and his rival Escamillo

Posters for *The Gold Rush* (1925)

and *Monsieur Verdoux* (1947)

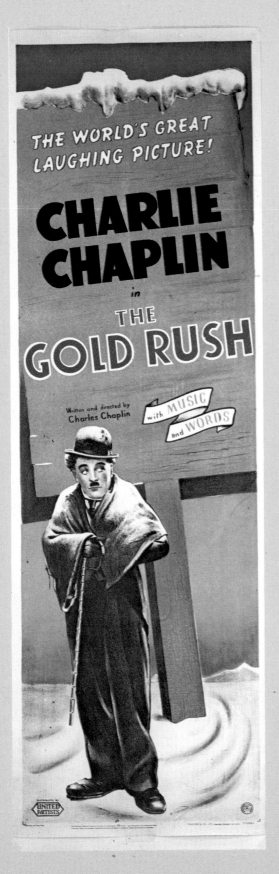

THE WORLD'S GREAT
LAUGHING PICTURE!

CHARLIE
CHAPLIN

in

THE
GOLD RUSH

Written and directed by
Charles Chaplin

with MUSIC
and WORDS

DISTRIBUTED BY
UNITED
ARTISTS

CHARLES
CHAPLIN
in
"MONSIEUR"
VERDOUX"

featuring MARTHA RAYE
and
Isobel Elsom · Marilyn Nash · Robert Lewis
Written and Directed by
CHARLES CHAPLIN
Associate Directors Robert Florey and Wheeler Dryden

UNITED
ARTISTS

duel with kicks and rubbery swords, age-old stage stuff topped by a visual gem when Charlie wraps a blanket around his shoulders, shrinks down inside, and scuttles away like a tent on wheels. The finale is unique. Like the original, the burlesque ends in tragedy. Charlie stabs Carmen, kisses her farewell, then stabs himself, falling across her body. Audiences still gasp: they came to laugh – it is they who have been stabbed. Enter Escamillo. A quick kick, then both Charlie and Edna sit up, laughing at the trick they have played on us. Charlie shows how the blade slides inside his dagger, and the iris closes on the biggest April Fool joke ever pulled.

Chaplin's contract was due for renewal on January the first, 1916. Spoor took that train again and offered him $350,000 for twelve more two-reelers. Chaplin, now a firm believer in the bonus sytem, agreed, provided Spoor handed him an extra $150,000 cash on the nail. Spoor took the next train back to Chicago; Chaplin was out of a job. His final film for Essanay was copyrighted on 27 March, advertised on 13 May as *Police! Police!*, and released on 27 May as *Police*.

Charlie, 'Once again in the Cruel, Cruel World', steps through the prison gates into the welcoming arms of Pastor Fred Goodwins, all beard and bible. 'Let me help you go straight', he implores, picking Charlie's pocket. When a genuine preacher appears spouting the same subtitle, Charlie whacks the bible out of his hands and chases him in fury. He and his old cell-mate do a burlesque burglary, straight out of Karno's *Dandy Thieves*. Their noisy break-in (in a silent film!) brings down Edna in her nightie. 'Let me help you go straight', she says: instantly Charlie claps his hands over his pockets! She gives him a coin, which he tests with a quick bite. That night at the doss-house his old partner creeps in to rob the inmates. Charlie scares him away by disguising himself as a monster and next day returns Edna's jewels. She is delighted: her true Christianity has reformed him. With arms outstretched ecstatically he flip-flaps down the road, only to be confronted by the cop who has been on his trail from the start. Charlie runs for it and the final iris closes down on the cop's face, not his. *Police* salts slapstick with irony, making a comment on society and the false face of charity.

The doss-house sequences, amusing but with a realism that only first hand experience could recreate, fit awkwardly into the comedy continuity. In fact they come from a film called *Life*, which Chaplin intended as his first full-length feature. Forced to abandon it by Essanay's insistence on maintaining regular releases, Chaplin used some of it to pad *Police* to two-reel length. Later Essanay took it out again, and with the rest of *Life*, some of *Work*, and some completely new material directed by Leo White, they were able to release a 'Brand New Charlie Chaplin'. *Triple Trouble* went out on 11 August 1918, two and a half years after Chaplin had left Essanay!

The Kid (1921) with Jackie Coogan

6
The Star Boarder
(1916-1917)

THE KEYSTONE FILM CO.

The Rink (1916) with Edna Purviance, Eric Campbell and Albert Austin

'I AM NOW WITH MUTUAL'
After thoroughly investigating the motion picture field, I have decided to affiliate myself with the Mutual Film Corporation. My future pictures will be released by Mutual exchanges because they serve the greatest number of exhibitors throughout the country.
                    Mutually yours, Charles Chaplin.

The announcement, 'the most gigantic in the history of the film industry', took up four pages of colour in *Moving Picture World* for 11 March 1915. Chaplin had arrived in New York on 14 February after a five day train trip punctuated by such riotous public demonstrations that the New York Chief of Police had cabled him to get off at the stop before Grand Central because of the crowd. Syd met him at the 125th Street station with exciting news. Ira Lowry of V.L.S.E. (a merger of Vitagraph, Lubin, Selig and Essanay) would meet them at the Hotel Astor. Lowry arrived while Chaplin was in the bath. 'I want ten thousand dollars a week', said Chaplin. Lowry agreed. But while V.L.S.E. discussed the deal, John R. Freuler, president of Mutual, who had been wooing Chaplin since July, stepped in. He met Chaplin's demand and added a cash bonus of $150,000. Claimed *Moving Picture World*, 'Never in the history of the stage and its related arts has there been a salary of this magnitude.'[47] Yet $670,000 was small beer when set beside Freuler's estimated takings, $2,200,000 for the year. Chaplin's first film for Freuler was released on March 9: item 14 of *Mutual Weekly No. 62*, a newsreel showing him signing the contract on February 26.

Henry P. Caulfield, Chaplin's new production manager, was sent to Los Angeles to locate a suitable studio. He found the Climax at 1025 Lillian Way in Hollywood. Chaplin renamed it the Lone Star, for so he was. For the first time he had an entire studio to himself. He assembled a crew that was tried and true: Rollie became assistant to ace cameraman William C. Foster, while Edna and Charlotte Mineau were brought from Essanay, as were Bud Jamison, Jimmy Kelley, Frank Coleman, Lloyd Bacon, and Leo White. Leo, from Manchester, now headed a British contingent: Albert Austin from Birmingham, an old Chaplin 'oppo' from the Karno tours, and Eric Stuart Campbell from Dunoon. This towering Scot was spotted by Syd while playing *Pom-Pom* at Cohan's Theatre, New York. Recognizing his giant partner from his own Karno days, Syd signed him on the spot, seeing in him the perfect Goliath for his brother's David.

Chaplin was delighted to be thus surrounded by cheery compatriots; they made a great audience for the off-set antics which had become part of his movie-making routine. Out of his improvizings around the scenery and props came many of his finest on-screen moments. And when yet another refugee from the Karno Fun Factory turned up as bellhop in the

Los Angeles Athletic Club where he roomed, Chaplin immediately took him on his staff. Chester Courtney, clocking in at the Lone Star next morning, was surprised to find everybody idle. And they remained idle all week: Chaplin was awaiting inspiration.

'Then the Big Idea struck him accidentally. He was standing in Hamburger's Department Store, Los Angeles. The elevator was running. His eyes seized on it and remained riveted. His mind began to revolve. In it he saw himself at the head of a chase on the running stairway; he and his pursuers going down while the elevator rolled up. He ran to the phone. "Build me a moving stairway" he commanded.'[48] The giant prop became the core of *The Floorwalker*, Chaplin's first Mutual two-reeler. Eric Campbell, at his most beetling and bearded as the embezzling manager, led the chase. Carefully constructed, Chaplin's most expensively set film yet, *The Floorwalker* was all laughter and no heart. Edna appeared but briefly as Campbell's typist. She was at least the prime object in Chaplin's second Mutual, but again the film was little more than slapstick, although the inspiration came once again from his observation of life.

Charlie in the Café

'I was passing a firehouse one day, and heard a fire alarm ringing. I watched the men sliding down the pole, climbing onto the engine, and rushing off to the fire. At once a train of comic possibilities occurred to me. I saw myself sleeping in bed, oblivious to the clanging of the fire bell. This point would have universal appeal, because everyone likes to sleep. I saw myself sliding down the pole, playing tricks with the fire hoses, rescuing the heroine, falling off the engine as it turned a corner . . .'[49]

The Fireman follows Chaplin's instant scenario exactly, adding a great opening for Charlie: the alarm rings and Charlie, last to hear, is dressed, down the pole, and driving the horses up the street before he notices he has left Captain Campbell and crew behind! Chaplin's cops in *Police* had been the antithesis of Keystone's: they sauntered to the scene of the crime, not sped, and not until they had finished their tea. Chaplin's firemen were equally opposite: at the scene of the fire they first did their drill. But this burlesque ballet strikes false against the realistic backgrounds. Chaplin filmed in a genuine fire station, and two condemned houses were bought and burned to the ground for the climax. At Mutual's expense, of course. But what his first two Mutuals lacked in heart was more than made up for in his third.

The Vagabond begins with a shot of Charlie's world-famous feet, then the little Tramp shuffles into view through the swing-doors of a saloon. He starts a soulful solo on his fiddle (Chaplin's musicianship had lately been the subject of much publicity), but is forced to yield to a German band. Strange that a man whose country was two years into a war should so

above: *The Immigrant* (1917) with Eric Campbell, Edna Purviance and Henry Bergman

below: *A Night Out* (1915) with Ben Turpin and Leo White

unthinkingly use the enemy for casual fun (Chaplin's absence from his home had lately been the subject of much publicity, too). He wanders into a gypsy camp and saves Edna from the lash of Campbell the Chief. A country idyll ensues, with Edna posing for a passing painter while Charlie cracks eggs with a hammer and traps flies in his pocket. Mother Mineau sees the portrait on show and with a cry of 'That birth mark: my child!' locates her long-lost daughter. They drive off in a gleaming limousine, leaving a heart-broken Charlie. Then the car turns, Edna comes back for Charlie and together they drive down the road to love and riches.

The happy and dramatic ending replaced Chaplin's original. Charlie jumps in the river to drown his sorrows, is saved by Phyllis Allen, takes one look at her homely mug and jumps in again! By replacing farce with human happiness Chaplin showed a new maturity in his movie making. *The Vagabond* was contrived around an oil painting of Edna presented to her by a New York artist. The film also records Chaplin's social advancement. The Rembrandt in the gallery scene was loaned by his latest acquaintance, a local connoisseur. But for all the rich trappings and advancement in dramatic technique, *Variety* could still find fault: 'Right from the start you are shocked by an old burlesque bit. This refers to the picking up of an expectoration in mistake for a coin.' Neither did they like Edna indicating 'in pantomime that her cranium is populated with vermin'. And of course, it was no help that the hag he kicked in the belly was really Leo White in drag. Chaplin was still Chaplin, comedian of the people, and his comedy roots were as low as his own. But he was beginning to evolve, helped by the wealthy who sought his company, and the intellectuals who 'took him up'. The first was Minnie Maddern Fiske, who wrote on 'The Art of Charles Chaplin' in *Harper's Weekly* for May 6, 1916. 'Chaplin is vulgar', she declared, but pointing out his line of descent from such vulgarians as Aristophanes, Plautus, Terence, Shakespeare, Rabelais, Fielding, Smollett and Swift, she added 'Vulgarity and distinguished art can exist together'.

One A.M. surprised everyone, except those who had seen Billy Reeves' *The Clubman* fifteen months before, and those who had seen the Karno companies years before that. For Chaplin's much-acclaimed cinematic solo is no more than a flatly photographed vaudeville routine. Charlie, evening dressed and invernessed, is the classic drunken dude. He has one simple objective: to go upstairs and get to bed. But the entire house conspires against him: a fishbowl gets on his foot, a tigerskin rug bites his hand, a stuffed lynx snaps at his leg. The staircase makes him slip down so many times he has to tackle it with an Alpine kit. Worse trouble awaits him in the bedroom. Folded into the wall is a Murphy bed, an enemy more implacable, more violent, more unpredictable than any irascible Campbell or irate Count. A new kind of climactic battle begins, Charlie versus machine. The bed bashes him on the head, bucks him like a broncho, bears him into the wall, and just when Charlie seems to have mastered it, achieves victory in defeat by collapsing beneath him. As 'prop comedy' *One A.M.* topped them all until Buster Keaton emerged as master of malevolent machinery.

The Count is another harkback, this time to the Keystone formula of imposture. Charlie helps a clothes-presser, Campbell in incredible beard with eyebrows to match (the synopsis calls him 'Buttinsky the Nihilist'). Charlie has a naughty time measuring May White for a suit, and later indulges in another spot of favourite fun by getting his hand stuck in an over-ripe Camembert. This is while calling on the cook at the Moneybags Mansion, where he comes face to furious face with Campbell, posing as Count Broko. To save himself Campbell introduces Charlie as his secretary, and they sit down with Edna to a classic Chaplin meal: the way Campbell sucks up spaghetti is capped only by Charlie's way with watermelon. At the dance the real Count (Leo) arrives, the cops are called, Campbell is bowled over by cake, and Charlie runs, not walks, down the road to tomorrow.

The dance sequence took Chaplin three weeks to shoot, a hired orchestra playing all the while. 'If anyone were to play *They Call it Dixieland* in my hearing, I should run screaming!' wrote Chester Courtney.[48] He went on to describe how Chaplin held up work on his next film for two weeks while he learned to play all the instruments that his prop man, Scotty Cleethorpes, had provided as dressing for *The Pawnshop*. Then Chaplin gave his crew a concert, playing one tune on each instrument!

The Pawnshop turned out to be a minor masterpiece, founded upon Chaplin's janitor pictures but rooted in life: his audience knew well the pawnbroker's shop. He begins with the now traditional prologue: Charlie arrives, all brisk and business, sticks his cane down a trumpet, pops his bowler into a birdcage, and dusts the electric fan, filling the shop with feathers. Al Austin arrives to pawn an alarm clock and stands implacably by as Chaplin, in his most sustained single sequence ever, runs a gamut of gags until the timepiece is reduced to wriggling rubble which is swept into Al's hat and returned with a solemn shake of the head. The sequence is marred by one cutaway to the lugubrious Austin: Chaplin had had to either shorten the single-shot scene, or take out a gag that didn't come off. *The Pawnshop* was celebrated by the *Saturday Evening Post*: it gave Chaplin the cover.

Chaplin had freedom of creativity but was tied to time. He knew he could never make the better pictures his new friends were urging him to make whilst tied to the one-a-month Mutual schedule. With *Behind the Screen* he slipped so far

Charlie versus the Machine

above: *One A.M.* (1916)

below: *Modern Times* (1936)

back that they had to issue a special statement: 'This production is being made on such an elaborate scale that the release date will be postponed two weeks in order to complete it properly.'[50] When finally unveiled, the elaboration was more on Chaplin's earlier movie burlesques than on production qualities. Once again he was using his studio as a set.

Edna arrives at the Gigantic Picture Studios, hoping to be a film star. The answer is no despite her gesture, the finger-to-mouth pose that Chaplin had first used in *The Bank*, and which had become his all-purpose symbol of emotion. His other symbol, the working-man's pipe, is also in evidence, as we are introduced to Charlie and Campbell by subtitle as 'David and Goliath'. They are stagehands, bully and bullied, and at lunchbreak Charlie gets the full blast of Al Austin's onion. He wraps his dry bread round the end of Al's mutton bone to make a secret sandwich. When the rest of the stagehands strike, Charlie and Campbell hire a likely-looking lad, who turns out to be Edna. Charlie slips her a kiss, and Campbell, not in on the secret, squeals an effeminate 'Oh, mercy!' The custard pies get out of control, Campbell falls down a trapdoor, the strikers dynamite the studio, and Charlie and Edna wink at the camera in a climactic kiss.

above : *The Pawn Shop* (1916)

The Rink came as an eye-opener to those who had not seen *Skating*, the Karno sketch Syd had created and Chaplin had toured with. 'Everybody knows that Chaplin's feet are the funniest facts about Chaplin. Well, Charlie's feet with roller skates on them are funnier feet than ever!'[51] Charlie the waiter tots up Campbell's bill by a brisk once-over of the spots on his waistcoat: soup, 'spiggety', 'mellon' and four beers. He mixes a cocktail, adds an egg, then adds a carnation to counter the smell. He shakes it superbly, vibrating every part of his body *except* his hands! Once on skates he becomes surprisingly graceful; his cane comes in handy to trip Campbell when that fat flirt pursues pretty Edna. She invites him to her party that night. Charlotte Mineau brings Campbell, Edna's father brings Campbell's wife, and all collide with Charlie on the rink. Women scream, the cops arrive, and the chase ends when Charlie hooks his cane to a passing car and disappears down the street with a wave of his top hat.

Easy Street began as a set. The street scene, straight from the slums of Kennington, was sketched out by Chaplin, built under his orders at a cost of 10,000 dollars, then left standing while Chaplin made three other films. When at last the idea dawned, a true masterpiece was created. The opening title is 'The Lost Sheep': Charlie the tramp huddled in the winter wind. The sweet sound of singing wakes him and he shuffles into the welcoming warmth of the Hope Mission, Edna at the organ. Prayers from Edna touch Charlie's heart, and he reforms: he returns the collection box which he'd tucked down his trousers! 'Easy Street' says a subtitle, and so it is for Big Eric if

right and overleaf: publicity material for *Modern Times* (1936)

CHARLIE
Chaplin in
MODERN TIMES
Written, Directed and Produced
by CHARLES CHAPLIN
Released thru UNITED ARTISTS

not for the poor policeman he is bashing. A notice is put up, 'Policeman Wanted at Once', and Charlie applies. Neat in his new uniform he struts down Easy Street only to meet Big Eric. Charlie's confidence evaporates and he tries to phone for help, while Eric demonstrates his powers by bending a lamp-post. During the demonstration Charlie repeatedly clubs Eric's head; Eric fails to notice. Suddenly Charlie leaps on his back, jams his head in the lamp, and turns on the gas. When Eric's gang comes sneaking up behind Charlie, he has only to turn sharply to send them scuttling in fright. Charlie is cock of the walk. He accompanies Edna on an errand of charity. They visit a starving family of twelve; Charlie gives the little father a disbelieving look and a medal! Big Eric now revives, breaks his handcuffs and chases Charlie around the block, upstairs and down, in and out of windows, until Charlie drops a gas-stove onto his head! A Russian blackjacks Charlie and pops him down a coalhole. He lands on a dope fiend's needle, receiving an unexpected injection that imbues him with super-human strength. Thus, 'Love backed by Force/Forgiveness Sweet/Bring Hope and Peace/To Easy Street'. Window boxes bloom on Charlie's peaceful beat. Big Eric raises his bowler to Charlie and Edna as he strolls to the New Hope Mission, arm-in-arm with the wife. *Easy Street* was another late release, but this time the cause was more painful: the bendy lamp-post landed on Chaplin's nose and he had to take to his bed at the Athletic Club. His recovery gave him an idea for his next film, which he first called *The Health Resort*.

The Cure reintroduces Charlie the drunk, with wealth enough to take a cure for his alcoholism, and a straw hat on his head. Only his moustache and cane remain the same. He arrives at the Spring Hotel in a bathchair, and is soon entangled with the gout-ridden Campbell in a revolving door. Charlies spills the spring water on his knee and casts a reproachful eye at a nurse's toy dog by his side. In the Turkish bath, Campbell pulls aside a cubicle curtain, disclosing Charlie in a bathing suit, posing like Napoleon. A second swish of the curtains, and Charlie is posing as September Morn! Meanwhile Charlie's hidden store of liquor is thrown through the window. It lands in the hotel well. By the time the cured Charlie steps sober from his room, the hotel resembles a Bacchanalian orgy!

John Jasper, the Mutual manager, now hired Carlyle R. Robinson as Chaplin's press agent. He would stay with the star for sixteen years. The latest picture was a month late: Robinson soon found why. '*The Immigrant* had to be cut down to sixteen hundred feet. Forty thousand feet had been shot. For four days and nights, without rest or sleep, Chaplin milled in the film. When finally it had been cut his closest friend would not have recognized him. His hair was a matted mess. Collarless, haggard, and dirty. But his picture was finished.'[52]

The Gold Rush (1925)

The Immigrant has a fine opening gag: the back view of Charlie's familiar figure as he hangs over the rail of a swaying ship. Suddenly he straightens up: he was simply catching a fish. 'More rolling': but this time of dice. Charlie wins, and the bested gambler stomps away to steal a widow's sack of savings. Charlie consoles her weeping daughter, Edna, with his winnings. 'The Land of Liberty': the immigrants crowd the rail to glimpse the famous Statue, then are swiftly roped in like cattle by customs men. This became Chaplin's most famous gag, its implied comment appreciated by the rich, understood by the poor. 'Later – Hungry and Broke' Charlie finds a dollar and orders a plate of beans. Then he spots Edna. His bursting joy is stilled by the sight of a crumpled hankie in her hand: it has a black border. Again, unexpected understatement in a two-reel comedy. Now the waiter, Campbell at his most Campbellish, presents the check. Panic! Charlie has lost the coin! Here comes a third Chaplin classic as he invents delaying tactics, trying to get the dollar from under Campbell's foot. When at last he hands it over, Campbell tests it with his teeth: it bends. Luckily Henry Bergman, artist, chances past and hires Edna as a model. Charlie begs two bucks on account, then puts them to perfect use. They shelter from a storm in a door marked Marriage Bureau: Charlie carries his Edna over the threshold.

Chaplin was so exhausted by his cutting-room ordeal on *The Immigrant* that he declared a studio holiday. He and Syd disappeared to San Francisco for a week, then took the company to Sierra Madre where they began to shoot scenes on the sea shore. *The Convict* was begun as part of *The Immigrant*; now Chaplin developed it into *The Adventurer*. But it was a film dogged by ill-luck. They spent too long on location thanks to rough seas (but Chaplin actually rescued a small girl from drowning); then Edna fell ill and was taken to the Good Samaritan Hospital. Finally Chaplin ended up with 20,000 feet of film in the can!

The opening gag is Charlie's head popping out of a pile of sand. He is right next to the rifle of a slumbering prison guard, so he pops straight back in again! Charlie, a convict on the run, scoots up a cliff with help from Rollie's undercranked camera. Swiping a swimmer's clothes he saves Edna's mom from drowning and is invited to her stately home. In the morning his striped pyjamas and barred bed make Charlie think he is back in jail! As usual, a party is being flung, and as usual Charlie must pose as a society dude. Naturally Campbell is there and recognizes the convict from his picture in the paper. Charlie hides by putting a lampshade over his head and standing very still. Then he traps Campbell's head in some sliding doors, kisses Edna's hand, and is gone. It was Chaplin's last film for Mutual and Eric Campbell's last film ever. The old Goliath met his real life David in December 1917: he was killed in a car crash.

Charlie's Gesture
The Bank (1915)

Paulette Goddard in
Modern Times (1936)

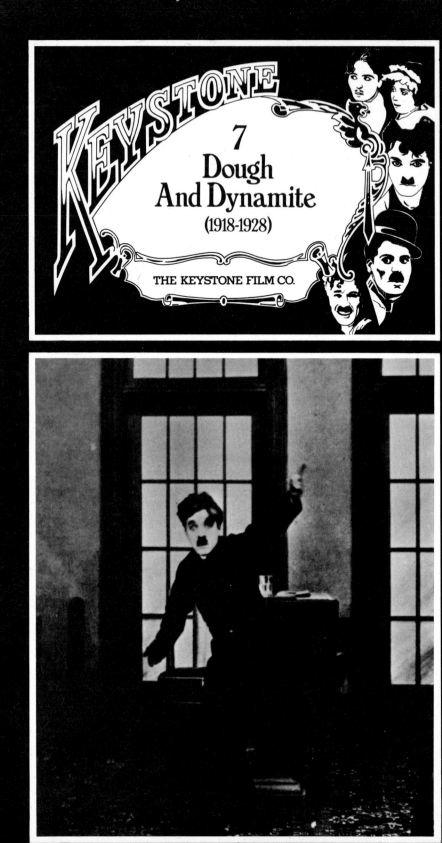

7
Dough
And Dynamite
(1918-1928)

THE KEYSTONE FILM CO.

CHAPLIN SIGNS WITH EXHIBITORS' CIRCUIT

Charlie Chaplin has contracted with the
First National Exhibitors' circuit to
produce eight pictures. He is to receive
a salary of $1,000,000 and a bonus of $75,000.

As *Moving Picture World* pointed out, $1,075,000 'is the highest salary ever paid a man in any walk of life for a like period of time'. They broke the news on July 14, 1917 while Chaplin was in the thick of his commitment to Mutual. Freuler had offered to renew at a million, Mutual bearing all production costs, but Chaplin wanted a studio of his own, and the new circuit, First National, gave him that chance. Its organiser, J. D. Williams, had been working on the deal since February, travelling America to sign 25 prominent exhibitors to an exclusive franchise arrangement, and extracting a levy from each to meet Chaplin's requirements. Chaplin was signed to deliver eight films in sixteen months. It took him five years.

First, Chaplin took Edna to Honolulu for a holiday while John Jasper, continuing as his general manager, looked after the construction of his new studio. He had acquired the five acre estate of R. S. McClellan on Sunset Boulevard: the ten-room Colonial house to the north would be retained as his home, while he instructed Myer and Holler of the Milwaukee Building Co to design the studio to blend with the bungalows of his millionaire neighbours.

The gap between new Chaplin films had been steadily increasing, from the weekly Keystones to the monthly Mutuals. Only the first nine of his Lone Stars had come out on cue; the last three stretched the schedule from two months to four. With six months to wait before the first 'Million Dollar Chaplin', small wonder rival producers rushed in to satisfy exhibitors' demands. Spoor and Anderson were first in the field with their *Essanay-Chaplin Revue of 1916*, which stuck together extracts from *The Tramp, His New Job*, and *A Night Out*. In England, Langford Reed the Limerick King constructed *Chase Me Charlie* out of the same Essanays, hiring an impersonator, Graham Douglas, to fill in a few linking scenes. Premiered at the Stoll Picture House, Kingsway, its first week's audience numbered 30,000! There would be many such compilations down the years, especially after the talkie revolution allowed the introduction of music and sound effects, but none of them compare with the one Chaplin himself made. In 1959 he fashioned *The Chaplin Revue* from three of his best First Nationals, *A Dog's Life, Shoulder Arms* and *The Pilgrim*. As with its predecessors, it did as well with the public as would have a brand new Chaplin feature.

Sennett, as early as 1914, had publicly threatened the law on print pirates who duped Chaplin Keystones and put them out under new titles. Now he joined in the game, reissuing the old

films with new sub-titles written by Syd Chaplin. Those films he had neglected to copyright were anybody's game, and company after company put them on the market under new titles as 'New Chaplins'. Later the same thing happened to the Essanays and Mutuals; as late as 1927 these were reissued in England as new comedies with new sub-titles designed by Tom Webster, the sports cartoonist. With his First National deal, Chaplin was able to hold on to his copyrights, and from this time all revivals have been strictly under his personal supervision.

The impersonators, meanwhile, rolled merrily on, the two Billies being augmented by the third and best, Billy West. A young Oliver Hardy played Billy's Goliath. In England, the Neptune company cast burly John M. East as Swain-Campbell and John Collins as Charlie in *Chicken Hearted*. In Australia, Ern Vockler was *Charlie at the Sydney Show*. France had André Séchan as 'Monsieur Jack', Germany Ernst Bosser as 'Charlie Kaplin'. But when Mexican comic Carlos Amador changed his name legally to Charlie Aplin, it was too much. Chaplin sued and won. The only movie maker who really got away with it was Pat Sullivan: for Universal he animated a whole series of Charlie Cartoons.

Charlie in Disguise

With so much imitative activity no wonder Chaplin opened his first 'Million Dollar' release, *A Dog's Life*, by scrawling his autograph: 'None genuine without this signature'. Dawn rises on Charlie, huddled by a fence with Scraps his 'thoroughbred mongrel', stuffing his hankie in a knothole to stop the draught. There is social comment in his opening sequence: at the employment office Charlie is shoved from window to window by desperate job-hunters: the last window is slammed in his face. In the animal kingdom Scraps has no better luck: he finds a bone but is instantly set on by all the starving dogs in the city. As Chaplin's first symbolic parallel it is superior to his juxtaposition of sheep and workers in *Modern Times*. There is a moral, too: teamwork pays. While Charlie chats up a grocer, Scraps swipes sausages; while the grocer watches Scraps, Charlie scoffs cakes! Scraps digs up a wallet buried by Al Austin and pal. Charlie repairs to the Green Lantern Café, where the crooks claim back their loot. Charlie stuns Al with a mallet, slips his arms through the dazed man's coat, beckons his buddy closer, then clouts him with a bottle. With Edna, a sacked singer, and Scraps at his heels, Charlie goes down the road to 'When Dreams Come True'. For the first time Syd appeared in a film with his brother. He played the proprietor of the lunchwagon in which Charlie is besieged by the thieves. As Chaplin's manager, Syd had little time now for performing, but managed to play two parts in the next picture, an American Sergeant and the German Kaiser.

Great Britain had gone to war with Germany in August, 1914, and there were many who considered Chaplin was shirk-

above: *Shoulder Arms*
(1918)

below: *The Gold Rush*
(1925)

ing his duty. The United States went to war in April, 1917, and even more thought the same. Carlyle Robinson, now his personal press agent, and Tom Harrington, his secretary, drafted a statement. Chaplin said 'I will willingly go when called . . . I have always considered that I have been doing my "bit" despite the fact that I am not in the trenches with a gun on my shoulder.'[52] And to show a willing face to the world, Chaplin went on a two month tour to sell bonds for the Third Liberty Loan. On 8 April 1918, 30,000 people packed Wall Street to see Chaplin, Mary Pickford, and Douglas Fairbanks promote bonds. Later, Chaplin was received at the White House, where he danced again with dear old Tillie, Marie Dressler. He made a short film for the Liberty Loan Committee in which he belted Kaiser Bill with a mallet marked 'Liberty Bonds'. It was not all one way; his tour of Southern training camps gave him the idea for his next film.

Shoulder Arms introduces conscript Charlie as a member of 'The Awkward Squad': naturally with his feet more awkward than most. Exhausted by drill he flops on his cot, and when next seen is 'Over There'. The trenches are posted 'Broadway' and 'Rotten Row', a sign of Anglo-American co-operation. 'News From Home': but there is no letter for Charlie. Then a parcel arrives for him. Typically it turns out to be that familiar limburger. Charlie whips on his gasmask, then flings the cheese so far it lands in a German's face! 'Bedtime': the dugout is flooded. Charlie submerges into sleep with the help of a phonograph horn.

'Over the Top' heralds the first Chaplin gag to depend on words not pictures. Charlie captures a line of Germans with the classic explanation: 'I surrounded them!' Then it is back to sight gags with Charlie in his craziest costume yet: he is camouflaged as a tree! He rescues Edna from the Jerries and captures Kaiser Bill himself, driving to the Allied lines in his staff car: 'Bringing Home the Bacon'. Carried on his cheering buddies' shoulders, Charlie wakes as they shake him on his boot camp cot. It was all a dream! Except in Chaplin's intended ending. There it was all true, with Charlie banqueted at the Palace of Versailles and making a speech of thanks while George V snips off a button for a souvenir! Planned as his first five-reel feature, Chaplin cut it short both to satisfy First National and to obtain a speedy release. He had spent so long making it that the war was almost over. It beat the Armistice by only one month. Despite its tardy topicality and its choppy continuity, *Shoulder Arms* was hailed by both press and public as Chaplin's best yet.

Press and public soon had something else to excite them. Twenty-one days after *Shoulder Arms* went on release, Charles Spencer Chaplin, aged 29, was married to Mildred Harris, 16, by the Reverend James Myers. The loving couple spent a quick week's honeymoon at Catalina, then settled into a new house at 2000 Catalina Drive, Lachman Park in North Hollywood. It was Chaplin's first home of his own. Little Mildred had been playing in pictures since she was ten, yet it would still be Edna who co-starred with Chaplin in his next film. If romance had too soon vanished in real life, then Chaplin could create it in the fantasy world of cinema. He would turn away from the war-shattered mood of today into the nostalgia of remembered yesterday. He would create a romantic idyll.

Sunnyside is set 'Some Years Back'. Charlie is Hired Man at the Hotel Evergreen, where the Hard Hearted Boss so over-works him that he has devised a labour-saving system. Charlie milks the cow directly into the cups and holds the hen over the skillet to lay fried eggs. He so adores Edna the Village Belle that he lets his cows stray into church; one of them bucks him into a ditch. Here he dreams of Arcady, where bare-limbed nymphs lure him to dance. Charlie twists his curls into horns and plays a daisy like the Pipes of Pan. They perform a burl-esque ballet, Chaplin's on-screen answer to Njinsky, who had visited Chaplin on the set of *The Cure* and told him, 'Your comedy is balletique; you are a dancer'. Later Charlie's real-life dream is broken when a City Slicker makes a play for Edna. Charlie tries to out-dude him, improvizing smart cuffs with paper, spats with socks, and a lighter in his cane with a candle. Edna laughs at him and Charlie throws himself under an auto. Then he wakes again: it was another dream! The Slicker departs and Edna is Charlie's! The dream ending, a favourite device, is even more effective for being used twice.

Sunnyside was released on 4 June 1919. One month later Chaplin's first child was born. Norman Chaplin, born deformed on July the seventh, died on the tenth. His tomb-stone reads 'The Little Mouse'. Mrs Chaplin moved to 674 South Oxford Drive and Mr Chaplin went back to the Athletic

right: *The Adventurer* (1917)

left: *Sunnyside* (1919)

P-3

THE LITTLE MAN WITH THE BIG HEART..

Charlie Chaplin

ALL IN COLOUR

No.1

PACKED
MAN
OF

6p

No.6 (New Series)Vol.1
DECEMBER 9, 1933

Malcolm Campbell's Mightiest Moment

PICTORIAL

Weekly 2d

EVERY FRIDAY

Why Chaplin Can't Laugh

THE FUNNY MEN!

Liberty

WINTER

THE NOSTALGIA MAGAZINE

STARRING
Milton Berle
Danny Kaye
Fibber McGee
and Molly
Bob Hope
Fred Allen
Jack Oakie
Will Rogers
Jack Benny
Fanny Brice
Burns and Allen
J-J-Joe F-Frisco
Laurel and Hardy
Charlie McCarthy
The Marx Brothers
Abbott and Costello

EXCLUSIVE:
THE PRIVATE LIFE OF CHARLIE CHAPLIN
by his press agent and close friend

OCTOBER 1972

M COMMEN

BIMONTHLY

Chaplin · John Wayne · Schaffner

John Simon · Stanley Kauffmann · Robin Wo

Charlie on the Cover

The face that sold a million
mags

Charlie and the Kids

right: *His Trysting Place*
(1914)

overleaf: *The Kid* (1921)
with Jackie Coogan

Club. Tom Geraghty, who wrote screenplays for Douglas
Fairbanks, took the dejected comedian to see the Annette
Kellerman show at the Orpheum. In it was an eccentric
dancer. He was no great shakes, but when he took his bow, a
miniature double took the bow with him, burst into a quick
tap, and ran off waving. The audience roared into applause. So
did Chaplin: he was seeing himself, the clog-dancing kid! The
idea came at once. The boy was a miniature of his dad; in a film
he could be a miniature Charlie! Chaplin was inspired, anxious to get back to work. And so Jackie Coogan, in derby hat
and baggy pants, played Charlie's son, the son Chaplin had
never had, in *A Day's Pleasure*.

Basically an improvised movie on Keystone lines, *A Day's
Pleasure* was made in a hurry to meet First National's needs.
But it did more: it helped Chaplin forget his unhappy marriage
and gave him a reason for living. While he was working he was
creating something more than mere movies; he was creating
life as he wanted it to be. Life with laughter and love, dreams
and hope, poverty and cruelty, but where there was always a
happy ending, if nothing more than a walk down the road to
tomorrow. In the false world of the film studio, his son was
not dead; he was a ready-made four-year-old called Jackie
Coogan. For him, around him, Chaplin created a story that
became so real to both of them that the film, when it finally
emerged after fourteen months gestation, became an instant
classic of the cinema. Two months before that première,
Chaplin and Mildred were divorced.

The Kid, 'A Picture with a Smile and Perhaps a Tear', opens
with Edna leaving a charity hospital, her baby in her arms:
'Her Only Sin was Motherhood'. The scene dissolves to a
painting of Christ carrying the cross (this symbol, often misunderstood, means no more than 'the cross she has to bear').
Edna stops to watch a sad young bride on the arm of her elderly

groom. Petals dropping from the bride's bouquet are crushed beneath the old man's shoe. Edna scribbles a note and leaves her baby on the back seat of their car. Thieves steal it, and dump the baby beside a dust bin. Down the alley strolls Charlie the Tramp, suavely selecting a dog-end from his sardine-tin cigarette case. He hears a feeble cry. Five years later, father and son set off to work. Their pattern is simple: the Kid breaks a window throwing stones, Charlie chances by in his trade of glazier, and repairs the damage for a price. Meanwhile, Edna has become a prima donna, using her money to help the poor. She gives the Kid a toy, little realizing he is her own son. She meets her betrayer again, too, but there is no reconciliation; a symbolic book entitled *The Past* opens to the page called 'Regrets'. Then the Kid falls sick. A van from the County Orphan Asylum arrives, and the Kid is carried away screaming. Charlie grabs him and they escape to a dosshouse, Charlie sneaking the Kid through the window. The proprietor discovers him and takes the sleeping Kid to the police. Charlie wakes, and his frightened shouts for the Kid are the loudest sounds in silent movies. He searches the streets until he falls exhausted to dream a dream of Heaven. It is the fairy place of a child's imagination: everyone wears white nightgowns and wings, and even the local bully can fly. 'Sin Creeps In': devils tempt, feathers fly and so does Charlie, but the Heavenly Cop shoots him down. He wakes to find the same Cop shaking him. The Cop takes him to a car, the car takes him to a house, and Charlie enters his true heaven: through the door into the waiting arms of Edna and his Kid.

This was more than just a film, it was biography. The slum and the attic were those burned for ever into the brain of the boy Chaplin. And, of course, the Kid *was* the boy Chaplin. Jackie's father had trained him in timing; he could mimic the stars of the day. Thus, under the repeated rehearsals of a magnetic and sympathetic actor-director, and blessed by a big-eyed cuteness that would melt any heart, Jackie Coogan turned in the greatest juvenile performance in cinema. Chaplin shot 400,000 feet of *The Kid*: 50,000 on one scene alone – the classic blanket bit. He edited it in secret, in a hotel room in Salt Lake City, for fear First National might attach the negative. They had refused to pay more than their contract specified: a total of $405,000. The film had cost Chaplin $500,000 to make. In the end they gave him $600,000 plus a cut of the gross; Chaplin made more than a million.

He used some of it to bring his mother to America. Tom Harrington was sent to escort her from London. Hannah, fresh from the Institution, was fine until the immigration authorities began to examine her. Recalled Rollie, 'They said "Are you the mother of Charles Chaplin?" And she said, "I'm the mother of Jesus Christ".' They detained Hannah at Ellis Island, and only when Chaplin guaranteed that she would

never be dependent upon the state did they allow her to enter *The Immigrant*'s 'Land of Liberty'. Charlie and Syd met her at Pasadena. The change in the ten years between was terrible. She was never to know what her boy had become. But she called him 'The King'.

Condé Nast, the publisher, was celebrated for his parties. Chaplin was always a welcome guest, and in return he christened his next film after Nast's high-tone magazine, *Vanity Fair*. Thackeray lovers misunderstood, and their pressure made Chaplin change it to *The Idle Class*. It is part of his comment that it is never clear which class is idle: wealthy Edna and her drunken hubby who ride in the Pullman, or Charlie the Tramp who rides under it. Once again Chaplin takes on both roles, a polished-up version of Pest and Rowdy; both ends meet at Edna's costume ball. More may be read into the intercut of the opposite Charlies than Chaplin intended, for 1921 was the height of his hobnobbing with intellectuals of all persuasions, and when the press's favourite question was 'Are you a Bolshevik?'

Chaplin was starting to make a film about plumbers when, quite suddenly, he walked off the set and went home – first class on the *Olympic* to 3 Pownall Terrace. If ever he had had doubts that the shadow of a tramp could be worshipped by the world, they were shattered by the incredible demonstrations of joyous adulation that greeted his fleshly coming. To have left Kennington an unwanted workhouse urchin, to return so rich, so loved, in so few short years, was enough to turn the brain of an ordinary mortal. It was the same story in France, in Berlin and back across America: whatever Chaplin did or said made headlines. On the way he turned it all into a book, 'ghosted' by Monta Bell. In America it was called *My Trip Abroad*, in Britain *My Wonderful Visit*.

Back in his studio Chaplin summoned up his staff and set to work on what would become his last two-reeler. He had made fun of the leisured class, now the working man would be his target. *Pay Day* opens with the sub-title, 'Hard Shirking Men'. Charlie is so slow with his shovel that the foreman (welcome back, Mack Swain) sends him up the scaffolding. Here in the heights he lays bricks with great speed, thanks to Rollie's undercranking. Staggering home drunk in the rain, Charlie catches a crowded streetcar and straphangs on his neighbour's braces. He falls out, taking the man's trousers with him, climbs into a lunchwagon and straphangs from a sausage! Home at last he oils his shoes but still arouses his wife (welcome back, Phyllis Allen).

Chaplin was now living in a rented house on Beechwood Drive. His parties were frequent, his guest list legend. When Lord and Lady Mountbatten came to stay, Chaplin made a private film with them: *Nice and Friendly*. And after supper they would all play 'Charlie's Game'. Each player drew a character to impersonate and an incongruous subject upon which to speak. Once Chaplin preached an impromptu silent sermon on David and Goliath; it became the core of his next film.

The Pilgrim opens with a joke that was old when the movies were young: an escaped convict changes his stripes for the clothes of a swimming minister. Charlie, of course, is the convict again: as a parson, he spots a Sheriff and automatically holds his hands out for the cuffs. The gesture is mistaken for a greeting by a reception committee awaiting a new minister, and he finds himself ushered to church. He arouses suspicion by the way he hefts the collection box, then allays it with his long and brilliant mime of David and Goliath. Later, at the home of Edna the organist, an old cell-mate breaks in to steal mother's mortgage money. Charlie, reformed by love, silently duels him, only to be arrested. But Edna's pleas are heard, and the Sheriff escorts Charlie to the Mexican border. He skips across; then bandits open fire. Faced with the choice of law to the left and lawlessness to the right, Charlie takes the middle way out. With one foot in each country he flaps into the future. This famous finale, always a big laugh and always considered more than a mere joke, becomes with hindsight the pre-echo of Chaplin's most famous statement. At the height of his rejection by the United States he said, 'I am a citizen of the world.'

The Pilgrim was completed on September 25, 1922. At last Chaplin was free to make films for United Artists, a corporation he had helped create in April 1919. Initiated as a gag to upset a projected merger of production/distribution interests, this combination of top stars and directors became fact under William C. McAdoo and Oscar Price. 'The lunatics have taken charge of the asylum' said Richard Rowland, head of Metro. Chaplin's fellow lunatics, Mary Pickford, Douglas Fairbanks, and David Wark Griffith, were none too pleased with his tardy completion of his First National contract. Indeed Chaplin offered them $100,000 for his release, but they refused. When in 1923 Chaplin finally delivered his first film to them, they wished they had accepted! Instead of comedy, it was drama; instead of starring Chaplin, it starred Edna Purviance; instead of helping the ailing U.A. by making the expected fortune, it was a disastrous flop. It was contrived to make a world star of Edna Purviance; she was virtually never seen on the screen again. It was one year in production, nine months in actual shooting, cost $800,000, and is the only Chaplin film he has never reissued. But it made an international star of the hitherto-villainous Adolphe Menjou, established Chaplin as a director of genius, and inspired Ernst Lubitsch to launch a whole new school of sophisticated cinema. The story was inspired by Chaplin's chance and exciting meeting with the extraordinary Peggy Hopkins Joyce. He called it *Destiny*, then

Public Opinion, and finally *A Woman of Paris*. Sub-titled 'A Drama of Fate', the film begins with less a foreword by Chaplin the writer than a statement by Chaplin the human being.

> Humanity is composed not of heroes and villains, but of men and women, and all their passions, both good and bad, have been given them by God. They sin only in blindness, and the ignorant condemn their mistakes, but the wise pity them.

Marie StClair (Edna), 'A Woman of Fate', plans to elope, but her lover's father is so shocked that he dies from a stroke. Marie takes the train alone. A year later she is the mistress of Pierre Revel (Menjou), 'Richest Bachelor in Paris'. She goes to a wrong address and has an embarrassing encounter with her old love and his mother. She hires him to paint her portrait, posing in her fine feathers. Jean paints her as he knew her, in a plain country dress. He promises his mother he will not marry Marie. Heartbroken, she returns to Pierre. Jean follows, there is a scene, and a shot rings out. Jean falls into a fountain, a suicide. His mother takes his revolver and sets out to kill Marie. Finding her weeping beside Jean's body, she lowers the gun. 'Time is a Great Healer': Marie is living in the country with Jean's mother. By chance Pierre and a friend drive through: 'By the way, whatever became of Marie StClair?' Pierre shrugs, and their car roars past a haywagon. On the rear ride an accordion player, a little boy, and Marie. They are singing . . .

Chaplin's original film ended with Marie's return to Pierre after Jean's suicide. U.A. preferred a more upbeat, more 'moral' ending, and the original was seen only in Europe. Although the film seems more subtitle-bound than necessary, Chaplin sought to tell his story visually wherever possible. Gone were the pictorial symbols of *The Kid*, to be replaced by subtle, unemphasized suggestion: the departing train is seen only as lights flashing across Marie's face; her relationship with Pierre is shown by a masculine collar tumbling from a drawer full of feminine frills; Edna's curvacious nakedness is outlined off-screen by the movements of her masseur's hands. Such visual touches not only delighted sophisticated critics, they deceived censors. Except in Pennsylvania, where the whole film was banned as 'indecent, immoral and dealing with prostitution'.

Chaplin spent a restful weekend at Pickfair, palace of those most united of artists, Mary and Doug. Naturally, they were anxious for him to begin his next feature for the Company. Chaplin hadn't an idea in his head. They sat looking through a stereoscope, a popular 3-D toy of the time. Among the views was one of the Chilkoot Pass, showing a long line of prospectors climbing the mountain in search of gold. In that instant a film was born.

Charlie does a dance

The Great Dictator (1940)

A Countess from Hong Kong (1966)

The Gold Rush began in March 1924, and Chaplin's co-star was the unknown Lita Grey. Unknown to the world, not to Chaplin; she had been his neighbour since she was seven. At twelve she had played the flirty angel in *The Kid*, at thirteen Edna's maid in *The Idle Class*. Then she was known as Lolita McMurray; soon she would be known as Mrs Charles Chaplin. On 24 November 1924 they married in Empalme, Sonora; she was sixteen, he was 35.

The Gold Rush began all over again. Chaplin's new co-star was another unknown. Georgia Hale's only role to date had been that of a poor dredger girl who had repulsed a white slaver in *The Salvation Hunters*. This low-cost slice of low-life had so excited Chaplin that he persuaded his partners to buy it for distribution. It was the first film directed by Josef von Sternberg. *The Gold Rush* went on location to Nevada, where with hundreds of extras Chaplin reconstructed Doug's stereoscope view of the Chilkoot Pass. It was Keystone methods gone mad: Chaplin, with no conception of plot, let the scenery stimulate his creativity. So much footage was shot that the final bill after fourteen months' production was estimated at one million dollars. In the end Chaplin got it all back, plus more than a million over. He also got a masterpiece; as he put it, 'This is the picture I want to be remembered by'.

The Gold Rush is set in the Klondike of 1898: Chaplin's first period picture. 'Three days from anywhere – a Lone Prospector', swinging his cane and flatfooting through the snow, unaware of a bear behind. He arrives at the cabin of Black Larsen, who orders him out. The wind blows him back in. It also blows in Big Jim McKay (big Mack Swain), who has just struck gold. It blows out Black Larsen. 'Thanksgiving Dinner': Charlie dishes up boiled boot. They tuck in, Charlie twirling the laces on his fork like spaghetti, sucking the nails like bones, offering Big Jim a pull of one bent like a wishbone. Of all his many meal scenes, this is Chaplin's classic. The hilarity is touched with humanity, for they eat Charlie's own boot. He must now wear a bundle of rags and sleep with his foot in the oven! Jim, starving again, 'sees' Charlie as a giant chicken, and chases him with a chopper. Charlie arrives at a boom town. In the Monte Carlo saloon he falls in love with Georgia, a dancing girl. He invites her to dinner on New Year's Eve. Charlie dozes off and dreams the party is on; spearing two rolls with forks, he makes them dance the Oceana Roll. Midnight, and the shoot-up celebration at the saloon wakes Charlie. He shuffles up and looks sadly through the window at Georgia singing 'Auld Lang Syne'. He is cheered by running into Big Jim. He has lost his memory and promises Charlie a fifty-fifty share if he will help him find his mine. They locate their old cabin, but while they sleep the big wind blows again. This time the entire cabin shifts, and ends up perched on the brink of an abyss. Charlie opens the door to

The Circus (1928) with Henry Bergman

Charlie's Love Look

Number one of *The Picture Show* (1919)

investigate and falls. He clambers back in, the floor tips up and he shoots through the door again. Eventually Jim climbs to safety and finds his lost gold. 'Homeward Bound on the Good Ship Success': Charlie caps his fortune by meeting Georgia.

The Gold Rush was previewed in June, 1925. On the 28th the Chaplin's first child was born and christened Charles Spencer; nine months and two days later came Sydney Earle Chaplin. The third Chaplin production of this interregnum was still-born: *A Woman of the Sea*, written by Chaplin, co-directed with Josef von Sternberg, starring Edna Purviance, has still not been shown. On 1 December 1926, Chaplin came home exhausted, found his house full of drunks, and ordered them out. Lita and the babies went, too, and on 10 January 1927, she filed suit for divorce. Her charges were horrible. So, in a different way, were those brought by the U.S. Government. Chaplin was dunned for $1,133,000 unpaid income tax!

Chaplin had been working on a version of *The Suicide Club* by Robert Louis Stevenson. Now he switched to a *Pagliacci* theme. The critics' praise for his pathos and scorn for his slapstick seemed to suggest that a legitimate combination of the two emotions might by found in the *Pagliacci* story of 'Laugh Clown Laugh'. He hired a real circus and menagerie and improvized his comedy bits around them. They remained on his payroll for a year, resulting in a movie that looked cheap yet cost more than the epic *Gold Rush*. Much of the delay was due to the emotional stress of the divorce: Chaplin suffered a nervous breakdown. Nor did it help that he was stuck with the inexperienced Merna Kennedy as co-star. She was a seventeen year old school chum of Lita Grey. But his choice of hero was all his own fault: Harry Crocker was the scion of a wealthy San Francisco family, hardly Rex the King of the High Wire, let alone a suitable co-scenarist and co-director.

The pathetic side of *The Circus* is pathetic in the wrong way. Charlie's heartbreak on hearing Merna loves Rex is mechanically done; there is none of the true feeling he had for Georgia. The finale, with Charlie helping the lovers marry, then sitting alone in the ring as the circus moves on, fails to touch the heart. The style of the film is as primitive as its plot. Rollie photographs the Ride for Life in three flat-on set-ups, robbing this high-spot of all its thrill. One has but to recall what Buster Keaton and Harold Lloyd were doing at the time to realize that already the art of cinema was passing Chaplin by. One suspects that some sympathy, even nostalgia, prompted the newly formed Academy of Motion Picture Arts and Sciences into honouring Chaplin at their first ever Academy Awards ceremony on May 16, 1929. He received a Special Award 'for versatility and genius in writing, acting, directing and producing *The Circus*.' One other Special Award was presented. It went to Warner Brothers for producing *The Jazz Singer*, 'the pioneer talking picture which has revolutionized the industry.'

Charlie and *The Gold Rush*
(1925)

above left : the tipping cabin

below left : signing Lita Grey

above : the Chilkoot Pass

below : the starved Mack
Swain

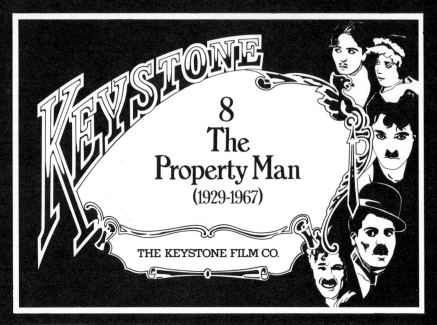

8
The
Property Man
(1929-1967)

THE KEYSTONE FILM CO.

'He Talks!'
United Artists advertisement for *The Great Dictator*

Chaplin spoke from the screen for the first time on 15 October 1940, exactly thirteen years and nine days after Al Jolson said 'you ain't heard nothin' yet'. In the years between Chaplin had made but two films – the last silent pictures ever made. Why did he cling to pantomime when the rest of the world's movie-makers rushed to get on the talkie bandwagon? It seemed particularly odd in view of his original misgivings about the silent screen. 'How could I give the effect of ripping my trousers without the 'r-r-r-r-rip' of a snare drum? When I slipped and fell on my head, how could the audience get the point without the loud hollow 'boom' from the orchestra?'[2]

The answer was twofold. First, Chaplin had matured with his movies, bringing the age-old art of pantomime to a peak of perfection and a world-wide appreciation never before known. This was the clue to the second point. Chaplin movies were truly universal; every country boasting a cinema showed them; all that was necessary was to translate the subtitles. Thus, as Syd was quick to point out, once Charlie talked this vast world market would be lost. And so in the March of 1928 Chaplin began to work on the only silent picture being shot in Hollywood. It was to be the perfect blend of pathos and pantomime: Charlie as a blind clown. But a piece of music was haunting Chaplin, *La Violetera*: 'Who'll buy my violets' would make a perfect theme song. And so a flower girl was born in his brain, and she became the blind one. A perfect part for the Edna of old, but now she was his pensioner.

One night at the fights Chaplin thought he saw the young Edna sitting opposite him. And so blonde, smiling, curvaceous, inexperienced Virginia Cherrill was signed up on the spot. Half a million feet of film later, Miss Cherrill was out and Georgia Hale was back in. Then Georgia went and Marilyn Morgan (age sixteen) arrived. But Marilyn went too, and so did Harry Clive, who was playing the important role of the Millionaire. He was replaced by comedy veteran Harry Myers, and she was replaced by – Virginia Cherrill!

On 28 August 1928 Hannah Chaplin died. Charlie arrived at Glendale Hospital too late for a last word, and Syd was filming in Elstree, England. She was buried close to the Little Mouse. After three years in production, the new film had an all-star premiere on 6 February 1931. There was music but no dialogue: 'And it's just as well because if the picture had had words, the laughs and applause of last evening's audience would have drowned them out.'[53]

City Lights, 'A Comedy Romance in Pantomime', opens as a monument to Peace and Prosperity is unveiled: it reveals the Tramp asleep in the statue's lap! As the National Anthem sounds, Charlie jumps to attention – and in classic reprise of one of his earliest comedy gestures, the statue's hand thumbs Charlie's nose! 'Afternoon', and the girl offers Charlie a flower. He realizes she is blind, gives her his last coin, and sits silently by in adoration. She empties a bucket of water over him! 'Night', and a drunken Millionaire, a millstone about his neck, determines to drown himself. Charlie intervenes, and like the Rounders of old, the two hie to a nightclub. The Girl falls ill, and to pay for a doctor, Charlie becomes a street cleaner. He takes the Girl food, and reads to her about a Viennese doctor who can cure blindness. 'Wonderful! Then I'll be able to see you.' Her excitement gives Charlie pause. To keep up the pretence of riches, Charlie turns boxer. The match is a balletic apotheosis of all Chaplin's boxing burlesques, but despite the aid of invisible wires, this time Charlie gets the K.O. The Millionaire, drunk again, gives Charlie the money for the operation. Unfortunately, a blow from a burglar sobers him up; Charlie gets the cash to the girl just before the cops catch him. He comes shuffling out of jail, a tattered tramp. There, looking and laughing at him through her flower shop window, is the Girl. She gives him a flower and puts a coin in his hand. The touch is terribly familiar. 'You?' she asks. He nods; 'You can see now?' 'Yes I can see now'. Charlie puts his finger to his mouth. Never has Chaplin's simple gesture been more fraught with meaning. His close-up fades to black: The End – one of the classic climaxes of all cinema.

City Lights was the first Chaplin film to be shown throughout the world exactly as its maker intended. Although he had personally selected the music to accompany all his pictures since *The Kid*, after the première his cue sheets could be ignored. The films could be accompanied by anything from a full-blown orchestra to a tin-pan piano. Now the much-despised soundtrack at least gave Charlie the right to impose his own musical standards. For three months he laboured to compose a score using *La Violetera* and other familiar themes among the new. Then he synchronized his film by personally conducting the orchestra. The bill came to $80,000, a flea-bite beside the total cost of $1,500,000. In the end he profited by five million.

Chaplin now embarked on another trip abroad, ostensibly to appear at the London première of *City Lights*. He ended up by touring the world for fifteen months. If the 1921 trip proved his popularity, then the decade between had magnified it tenfold. Shaw and Einstein, Ramsay Macdonald and Lloyd George: the men he met make a catalogue of the top of their time. There were women, too: Sari Maritza, Betty Amann, and May Reeves who wrote a book about her experiences and her child who died. Chaplin met another girl when he got home to Hollywood; Pauline Levy, age twenty, divorcing from Edgar James whom she had married at sixteen. She had been a

Chaplin and the United Artists

above: with Douglas Fairbanks, Alexander Korda, Mary Pickford, Samuel Goldwyn and associates.

below: Chaplin's studio

chorine in Eddie Cantor's *The Kid from Spain* under the name of Paulette Goddard. Chaplin bought a boat, just to surprise her, and was so impressed by her gamine liveliness that he determined to fashion a film around her. Recalling a reporter's story of how Detroit factory belts reduced former farmers to nervous wrecks, Chaplin sat down to write his first proper screenplay. He called it *The Masses*, as Paulette's part grew changed it to *Street Waif*, and premièred it exactly five years after *City Lights* as *Modern Times*. Like his last film, it was silent save for music and effects, and thus seemed to belie its very title. But as the *New York Times* announced to a Depressed world, 'This morning there is good news. Chaplin is back again.'

'*Modern Times* is the story of industry, of individual enterprise – humanity crusading in the pursuit of happiness'; so runs Chaplin's foreword. The smallest cog in a factory, Charlie became one literally when he is caught up in the whizzing wheels of a monstrous machine. He is chosen to test a mechanical feeder and experiences his most horrendous meal ever. The revolving corncob is bad enough, but the machine goes mad and rapidly plies him with best Keystone pies! Back on the assembly line it is Charlie's turn to crack up. After a quick burst of ballet with his wrenches, he runs amok, tightening the foreman's nose and the buttons on a woman's bottom. He is discharged from the psychiatric ward, cured, but unemployed. Waving a red flag that dropped off a truck, he is mistaken for the leader of a Communist demonstration and is promptly jailed. Pardoned, Charlie and the Gamin set up home in a shack they call 'Paradise'; Charlie sleeps in the kennel. Wrapped in ermine the Gamin watches as Charlie puts on a hair-raising roller-skate act: blindfolded, he circles ever nearer the edge of a broken balcony. The Gamin gets a job dancing in cabaret. She gets Charlie taken on as a waiter. Told to sub for an absent singer, he improvises gibberish to the tune of *Titania*: the first time the sound of Chaplin's voice had been heard in a film:

> 'La spinach or la busho, Cigaretto toto bello,
> Ce rakish spagoletto, Ce le tu la tu la trois!
> Senora de la tima, voulez-vous la taximeter,
> Le jaunta sur la seata, Je le tu le tu le waaah!'

Charlie's future as a singing waiter seems assured, but then the welfare officers burst in. They want the Gamin. Charlie grabs her and they take to the road, that long, long road down which Charlie has so often walked. This time he is not alone.

Nor was he in life. Chaplin and Paulette took a boat to China and were married along the way. Oddly, neither made the fact public until the première of their second film together. United Artists had taken Britain's most successful film-maker, Alexander Korda, into their reorganized fold. Korda pointed out to his new partner that both Charlie Chaplin and Adolf Hitler shared the world's most famous moustache. Chaplin seized on the idea at once. A film featuring both characters could help him maintain screen silence: Hitler could rant in the waiter's brand of double talk, while Charlie could stay his silent self. This was in 1937 when so political a picture would have been courageous indeed, but the war had been on for a year and a month before the film was completed. In the interval the world had changed, and so had Chaplin's concept. 'I did this picture for the Jews of the world', he stated. And it was in this film that Chaplin broke his long silence. He had finally found something worthwhile to say.

The Great Dictator is a full talkie, yet it opens with the usual subtitles: 'This is the story of a period between two World Wars – an interim in which Insanity cut loose, Liberty took a nosedive, and Humanity was kicked around somewhat'. In 1918, conscript Charlie of Tomania takes over a plane for Schultz, a wounded pilot. Charlie notices the sun below him shining upwards. He takes out his watch: it stands upright! Water from his canteen pours up into his face! He is, of course,

Charlie in Love

below and left: *Modern Times* (1936) with Paulette Goddard

right: *City Lights* (1931) with Virginia Cherrill

flying upside down! He promptly crashes. While Charlie lies in hospital, his memory gone, in his homeland Adenoid Hynkel and the Double Cross party rise to power on a platform of 'Democratia schtunk, Libertad schtunk, Freisprachen schtunk!' Charlie returns to the Ghetto, where storm-troopers string him up from a lamp-post. He is saved by Schultz, the pilot whom he had saved during the war, now an important Party official. Hynkel orders 3,000 strikers shot ('I don't want any of my workers dissatisfied'), and when his henchman Garbitsch predicts the world will worshop him as a god, Hynkel is so delighted that he shins straight up a curtain! Then, to the Prelude to *Lohengrin*, he dances a ballet with the globe of the world. The Dictator of Bacteria, Benzino Napaloni (Jack Oakie), is invited to meet Hynkel. Despite the train continually missing the red carpet, and a duel for supremacy in ever-rising barber chairs, the rival dictators reach agreement: they will invade Austerlich together. But Hynkel is mistaken for the fugitive Charlie and arrested, while Charlie is mistaken for Hynkel and put in charge of the invasion. The little Jewish

barber steps to the microphone and speaks: 'I'm sorry but I don't want to be an emperor . . .' His speech is long and stirring: 'We think too much and feel too little . . . more than machinery we need humanity . . . so long as men die liberty will never perish . . . the Kingdom of God is within man . . . let us fight for a new world, a decent world that will give men a chance to work . . . in the name of democracy, let us unite!' The crowd cheers. Then Charlie speaks to his lovely Hannah (Paulette). 'Wherever you are, look up, Hannah. The clouds are lifting, the sun is breaking through . . . the soul of man has been given wings and at last he is beginning to fly. He is flying into the rainbow, into the light of hope, into the future . . . Look up, Hannah, look up!' And perhaps, somewhere, Hannah Chaplin heard . . .

Paulette Goddard got her divorce in Mexico in July, 1942, and on the 22nd of that month Chaplin made his first public call for the opening of a Second Front, a popular demand of the time to relieve Russia from German attack. The U.S. press, critical of Chaplin's politics, grew vituperative when once again his morals made the front page.

Joan Barry had come to Hollywood from Brooklyn in 1940. She hoped to become a film star; she became a waitress. J. Paul Getty, the oil millionaire, took her on a wing-ding to Mexico, where she met Tim Durant from United Artists. Durant introduced her to Chaplin in June 1941. Chaplin put her under personal contract and announced that his latest discovery would star with him in *Shadow and Substance*. Instead she brought a paternity suit on behalf of her child, a girl born on 2 October 1943. Meanwhile, Chaplin looked elsewhere for a leading lady. He saw Oona O'Neill, the seventeen-year-old daughter of the playwright, Eugene O'Neill. On 16 June 1943 at Carpinteria near Santa Barbara he married her. Chaplin was 54; he had finally found his Hetty. If Chaplin's love life was settled at last, not so his professional and personal life. A Konrad Bercovici sued him for plagiarizing his original idea for *The Great Dictator*. He tried to prevent the deportation of Hans Eisler, composer and ex-communist. Summoned to appear before the Committee on Un-American Activities, he refused, replying in writing, 'I am what you call a "peace-monger"'. On 12 June 1947, John E. Rankin demanded in Congress that Chaplin be deported. 'His life is detrimental to the moral fabric of America'. Chaplin's latest film had opened two months before. It had already closed.

The Great Dictator had marked the end of Chaplin's Charlie. The Little Tramp had been totally humanized into the Jewish barber; now Charlie had broken his long silence there was no more to say. Like so many creative artists before him, Chaplin felt he had outgrown his character. He must break the restrictions that the mute Little Fellow placed on his art. Having abandoned *Shadow and Substance* he cast around

Charlie Speaks

above : *The Great Dictator* (1940)

below : *A King in New York* (1957)

right : poster for *Limelight* (1952)

KINEMATOGRAPH WEEKLY, February 5, 1953.

A NEW MASTERPIECE OF LAUGHTER —
THE BIGGEST WINNER
OF THEM ALL!

Charles Chaplin's

HUMAN DRAMA

LIMELIGHT

co-starring
CLAIRE BLOOM
SYDNEY CHAPLIN
with
Nigel Bruce, Norman Lloyd, Buster Keaton, Marjorie Bennett
Produced, written and directed by Charles Chaplin

UNITED ARTISTS

Chaplin directing Sophia Loren

left: *A Countess from Hong Kong* (1966)

below: *A King in New York* (1957)

for another idea, one which would star himself as a comedy actor in his own right. Orson Welles, the Hollywood Wonder-kid, came to Chaplin with a daring proposal. He wanted Chaplin to act in a film Welles would direct. Even more daringly he wanted Chaplin to play the French mass-murderer, Landru. Chaplin was taken with the idea, but the thought of performing in another director's picture was too much. Taking Welles' basic suggestion, he began to write a screenplay, calling it *Lady Killer*. It emerged four years later as *Monsieur Verdoux*, with the subtitle 'A Comedy of Murder'.

Chaplin wrote the film an explanatory programme note: 'Von Clausewitz said that war is the logical extension of diplomacy; Monsieur Verdoux feels that murder is the logical extension of business.' He set his black comedy about a Bluebeard 'Somewhere in the South of France' during the thirties. He played dapper Henri Verdoux, a greying Adolphe Menjou, maybe even an ageing Max Linder. He introduces himself as a voice over his own tombstone ('1880–1937'), explaining that he married and murdered wealthy women purely to support his home and family. Verdoux is first seen snipping roses as behind him an incinerator smokes ominously. In it is his thirteenth victim. Needing more money he takes the train to yet another wife. He persuades her to close her account, then closes with her. Then he takes the train again (train wheels become a running gag), but this time the loud-mouthed Annabella (Martha Raye) proves a problem. Verdoux acquires some poison and picks up a street girl to try it out. Her sad story so touches him that he spares her, giving her some money instead. Years later a penniless Verdoux is almost run over by the street girl. She is now the 'friend' of a munitions manufacturer. Suddenly Verdoux is arrested, and the girl goes to his trial. She weeps when the prosecution calls him 'a cruel and cynical monster'. Speaking in his own defence, Verdoux claims that the world encourages mass killing: 'I am an amateur in comparison'. In the condemned cell a priest asks him if he has no remorse for his sins: 'Who knows what sin is, born as it is from Heaven.' And when the priest prays for God to have mercy on his soul, Verdoux replies 'Why not? After all, it belongs to him.'

A lot of comedy; a lot of philosophy. Chaplin had attacked formal religion before, of course, but never so directly. *Monsieur Verdoux* had echoes of *A Woman of Paris*, and not merely in its setting, an equally phoney France. It also influenced other movie-makers, notably Robert Hamer with his *Kind Hearts and Coronets*, but in its content, not its style. *Monsieur Verdoux* was certainly a film before its time; but it was also a film behind its time – in technique. Where basic filming had always been sufficient to catch on celluloid the old Charlie's fooling, something much more sophisticated was required to match the style of the new Chaplin's writing and

113

playing. He realized this himself, and hired the experienced, and French, Robert Florey to help him direct. But it proved too much of a strain on his ego, and he hamstrung Florey with his overriding control. There was also yet another 'great discovery' in Marilyn Nash, who played the street girl, and of whom little was subsequently heard.

Chaplin expected *Monsieur Verdoux* to gross twelve million dollars; it was taken off after six weeks. Perhaps because of pressure by the American Legion; perhaps because Chaplin was no longer Charlie. United Artists, deep in the red, had looked to *Verdoux* to save the company. Instead, in July 1950 Mary Pickford and Chaplin, last of the Artists, sold out.

Chaplin now began to write *Footlights*; eighteen months later he had a script 700 pages long plus a twelve minute ballet called *Death of Columbine*. There was the usual pathetic love story, but this time touched with truth: an old man (Chaplin playing 'himself' at 63) and a young girl (Claire Bloom in her first big part at 23). But there was laughter, too, in remembered bits from his vaudeville heyday. In fact, it was to be Chaplin's autobiography, as false as those early ones he had written, but as true in spirit as he could make it. He built London in his studio, a remembered London, of lodgings and pubs, gutters and music halls. Chaplin played Calvero the Tramp Comedian, an ageing star fallen from favour in the modern times of 1914. He was himself, but he was Charlie too, although he refused to wear the Tramp's familiar clothes.

above: *Monsieur Verdoux* (1947)

Limelight opens with Calvero, drunk but dignified, tottering home: the tipsy swell come true. He is pulled up by a bad smell. He raises his shoe to study the sole, then spots a towel stuffed under a door. Gas! Instantly sober he smashes the door, grabs a young girl off her bed, and carries her up to his attic to revive. 'Life must be enjoyed', he tells her, 'It is all we have'. Terry tells him why she wants to die: she is a dancer and her legs are paralysed. Calvero takes charge of her. He gets the chance to appear on the halls again, but his old-fashioned act is a disaster. In comforting him, Terry recovers the use of her legs. She gets a job dancing at the Empire, and gets Calvero the small part of a clown in the ballet. Postant, the impresario, not realizing who the old clown is, decides to replace him. Calvero, his heart already broken over Terry – he realizes the age-gap between them – disappears. He is discovered busking in the street. Postant stages a benefit show for him, and Terry persuades Calvero to make one last appearance. He does an act with his former partner, and their slapstick battle between fiddle and piano brings down the house. Calvero, bursting with excitement, takes an encore, but the strain is too great. He collapses. Terry dances for him as he lies smiling on a couch in the wings. Before she finishes the old clown is dead.

Limelight is Chaplin's longest film, almost two and a half hours. Too long for many, but not for Chaplin: 'Today there

is too much speed. I like to dally a little'.[54] But against the longueurs of his philosophical discourses may be set the brilliance of the comedy sequences. For the first time he introduces them legitimately: they all take place on the stage, separate from the story. Chaplin's solos are funny enough, but are overcast by the expertly timed double-act. It is his only appearance with Buster Keaton, whose life more closely paralleled Calvero's than did Chaplin's! Chaplin's theme song for the film 'topped the pops' around the world.

Mr and Mrs Chaplin and their four children (Geraldine, Michael and Josephine appeared in *Limelight*) left America for the royal première in London. The U.S. Department of Immigration gave them a six months permit. As they set sail a cablegram was delivered. Chaplin was barred from re-entry pending his appearance before an Inquiry Board to answer charges of a political nature and of moral turpitude.

Chaplin took Oona to see Pownall Terrace – just in time, it was about to be demolished. Then he sent her back to America to wind up his affairs. The Chaplins travelled to Paris, where he was made an Officer of the Legion of Honour, to Rome, and thence to Lausanne in Switzerland. Here they settled at the Manoir de Ban in Corsier, a village above Vevey. Chaplin met Kruschev and Bulganin, Nehru and Chou En-Lai; Oona gave birth to Victoria and Eugene and Jane and Annette and Christopher.

In 1957 Chaplin came over to England to make his first film in his native home. They refused to show it in America. *A King in New York* introduces the silver-haired, 68-year old Chaplin in his first 'straight' role. There are no comedy make-ups or eccentric costumes for King Shahdov of Estrovia, although Chaplin contrives several set-pieces of slapstick and sight gags. Forced to flee his small European monarchy when revolution breaks out, Shahdov escapes to the States. While he speechifies to the press about his warm welcome, officials briskly take his fingerprints: *The Immigrant*'s 'Land of Liberty' with an up-to-the-minute twist. Shahdov visits a night club where the jazz is so loud (he is seated under a cymbal!) that he must mime his wants to the waiter. For caviar his hands swim like a sturgeon, for turtle soup they crawl under a saucer. Ann Kay (Dawn Adams), a smart tele-personality, contrives to get Shahdov on her show. Overnight he becomes a national celebrity, and his principles are soon forgotten. To look younger than his years he has his face lifted: then suffers agonies trying not to laugh at a slapstick whitewash act (Lauri Lupino Lane and George Truzzi) lest his stitches burst.

The satire takes a serious turn when Shahdov encounters young Rupert McAbee (Michael Chaplin), whose parents are charged with contempt by the Un-American Activities Committee for refusing to betray their friends. Shahdov himself is

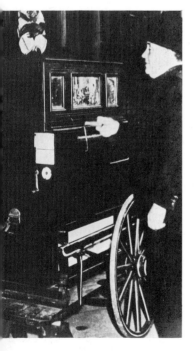

below: *Limelight* (1952) with Michael, Josephine and Geraldine Chaplin

summoned and accused of being a Communist. He gets his finger stuck in a fire hose and soaks the committee. Cleared, he learns that the boy has broken down and freed his imprisoned parents by betraying their friends. Rupert's spirit has gone, but wise old Shahdov assures him that with the fullness of time all will come right.

Chaplin, without his own studio and staff, without unlimited time and money, was revealed as an inadequate movie-maker by modern standards. Worse, without make-up he was an unfunny comedian. The hose-pipe gag was funnier when he first did it forty years before. Perhaps Chaplin should have walked down the road with Charlie, back in 1940. Certainly every time he reissued one of Charlie's old comedies with a newly composed music track, audiences flocked back in their millions.

above and right: *A Countess from Hong Kong* (1966)

A decade later Chaplin was back in a studio again and in England again. For the first time in 45 years he was making a film for a company that was not his own and in which he was not the star. *A Countess from Hong Kong* opens as ever, with a subtitle: 'As a result of two world wars, Hong Kong was crowded with refugees'. At the Palace of Beautiful Women, sailors with cash can dance with Countesses. The most glamorous of these, Natascha Alexandroff, finds herself dancing with Ogden Mears, American millionaire. When Ogden returns to his luxury liner he finds he has been appointed Ambassador to Arabia; he also finds the Countess in his closet. She tells him her sad story: daughter of Russian aristocrats, she fled to Shanghai. At fourteen she was a gangster's mistress. Natascha wants to go to the States, but has no passport. Touched, Ogden agrees to hide her in his suite. At every buzz of his bell a frantic hide-and-seek begins. To obtain American papers for Natascha, Ogden arranges a marriage of convenience with his effeminate valet. The 'first night' is a farce. At Honolulu, Ogden's wife Martha comes aboard; Natascha dives over the side. Their love is exposed. They finally reunite in a tango as the titles roll up.

A Countess from Hong Kong was difficult to make, technically (it was Chaplin's first film in colour and cinemascope) and artistically. He followed his method of acting out every part for his players, which hardly suited his star, Marlon Brando. Affronted by this apparent insult to his own method – 'The Method' – Brando let his displeasure show on the screen. His sullen performance as Ogden helped sink a story that should have bubbled like champagne. It even damped down the usually competent comedy of Sophia Loren.

Chaplin popped into the picture for a moment. As he had played a porter in *A Woman of Paris*, so here he played an ancient steward. He opens Brando's door, sways with seasickness, and closes it. He had no exit line. Charles Chaplin left films as he had entered them, in silence.

Chaplin Filmography

1914

Making A Living
2 February: (1030 ft): Keystone
Producer Mack Sennett *Director* Henry Lehrman
Screenplay Reed Heustis *Photography* E. J. Vallejo
Cast Charles Chaplin (Sharper), Virginia Kirtley (Girl),
Henry Lehrman (Reporter), Alice Davenport (Mother),
Chester Conklin (Cop), Minta Durfee (Girl)
Reissues A Busted Johnny; Troubles; Doing His Best;
Take My Picture

Kid Auto Races at Venice
7 February: (572 ft): Keystone
Producer Mack Sennett *Director* Henry Lehrman
Photography Frank D. Williams *Screenplay* Henry
Lehrman
Cast Charles Chaplin (Tramp), Henry Lehrman
(Director), Frank D. Williams (Cameraman), Gordon
Griffith (Boy), Paul Jacobs (Boy), Charlotte Fitzpatrick
(Girl), Thelma Salter (Girl)
British title Kid Auto Races
Reissues A Militant Suffragette; The Pest

Mabel's Strange Predicament
9 February: (1016 ft): Keystone
Producer Mack Sennett *Directors* Mack Sennett, Henry
Lehrman *Screenplay* Reed Heustis
Cast Mabel Normand (Mabel), Charles Chaplin
(Drunk), Chester Conklin (Husband), Alice Davenport
(Wife), Harry McCoy (Admirer), Hank Mann, Al
StJohn
Reissue Hotel Mixup

Between Showers
28 February: (1020 ft): Keystone
Producer Mack Sennett *Director* Henry Lehrman
Screenplay Henry Lehrman
Cast Ford Sterling (Masher), Charles Chaplin (Masher),
Emma Clifton (Girl), Chester Conklin (Cop), Sadie
Lampe (Girl)
Reissues The Flirts; Charlie and the Umbrella; In
Wrong; Thunder and Lightning

A Film Johnnie
2 March: (1020 ft): Keystone
Producer Mack Sennett *Director* George Nichols
Screenplay Craig Hutchinson
Cast Charles Chaplin (The Johnnie), Roscoe Arbuckle
(Fatty), Virginia Kirtley (Keystone Girl), Minta Durfee
(Actress), Mabel Normand (Herself), Ford Sterling
(Himself), Mack Sennett (Himself)
Reissues The Movie Nut; His Million Dollar Job

Tango Tangles
9 March: (734 ft): Keystone
Producer Mack Sennett *Director* Mack Sennett
Screenplay Mack Sennett
Cast Charles Chaplin (Drunk), Ford Sterling
(Bandleader), Roscoe Arbuckle (Clarinettist), Minta
Durfee (Cloakroom Girl), Chester Conklin (Dancer)
Reissues Charlie's Recreation; Music Hall

His Favorite Pastime
16 March: (1009 ft): Keystone
Producer Mack Sennett *Director* George Nichols
Screenplay Craig Hutchinson
Cast Charles Chaplin (Drunk), Roscoe Arbuckle
(Drunk), Peggy Pearce (Wife)
Reissues The Bonehead; Charlie's Reckless Fling

Cruel, Cruel Love
26 March: (1035 ft): Keystone
Producer Mack Sennett *Director* George Nichols
Screenplay Craig Hutchinson
Cast Charles Chaplin (Mr Dovey), Minta Durfee (Girl),
Chester Conklin (Butler), Alice Davenport (Maid)
Reissue Lord Helpus

The Star Boarder
4 April: (1020 ft): Keystone
Producer Mack Sennett *Director* George Nichols
Screenplay Craig Hutchinson
Cast Charles Chaplin (Boarder), Minta Durfee
(Landlady), Edgar Kennedy (Landlord), Gordon Griffith
(Son)
Reissues The Hash House Hero; The Landlady's Pet;
The Fatal Lantern

Mabel at the Wheel
18 April: (1900 ft): Keystone
Producer Mack Sennett *Directors* Mack Sennett, Mabel
Normand
Cast Mabel Normand (Mabel), Charles Chaplin
(Villain), Harry McCoy (Boy Friend), Chester Conklin
(Father), Mack Sennett (Rube), Al StJohn (Henchman),
William Seiter (Henchman)
Reissues His Daredevil Queen; A Hot Finish

Twenty Minutes of Love
20 April: (1009 ft): Keystone
Producer Mack Sennett *Director* Joseph Maddern
Story/Screenplay Charles Chaplin
Cast Charles Chaplin (Man), Minta Durfee (Girl),
Edgar Kennedy (Boy Friend), Gordon Griffith (Boy),
Chester Conklin (Thief), Joseph Swickard (Victim)
Reissues The Love Fiend; He Loved Her So; Cops and
Watches

Caught in a Cabaret
27 April: (2053 ft): Keystone
Producer Mack Sennett *Directors* Mabel Normand,
Charles Chaplin *Story/Screenplay* Charles Chaplin
Cast Charles Chaplin (Waiter), Mabel Normand (Girl),
Harry McCoy (Fiancé), Chester Conklin (Waiter),
Edgar Kennedy (Proprietor), Minta Durfee
(Entertainer), Phyllis Allen (Entertainer), Alice
Davenport (Mother), Joseph Swickard (Father), Gordon
Griffith (Boy), Alice Howell, Hank Mann, Wallace
MacDonald
Reissues The Jazz Waiter; Charlie the Waiter; Faking
With Society; Prime Minister Charlie

Caught in the Rain
4 May: (1015 ft): Keystone
Producer Mack Sennett *Director* Charles Chaplin
Story/Screenplay Charles Chaplin
Cast Charles Chaplin (Flirt), Alice Davenport (Wife),
Mack Swain (Husband), Alice Howell (Girl)
Reissues Who Got Stung; At It Again; In The Park

A Busy Day
7 May: (441 ft): Keystone
Producer Mack Sennett *Director* Charles Chaplin
Story/Screenplay Charles Chaplin
Cast Charles Chaplin (Wife), Mack Swain (Husband)
Reissues A Militant Suffragette; Busy As Can Be; Lady
Charlie

The Fatal Mallet
1 June: (1120 ft): Keystone
Producer Mack Sennett *Director* Mack Sennett
Cast Mabel Normand (The Girl), Charles Chaplin (The
Eccentric Rival), Mack Sennett (Her Adored One),
Mack Swain (The Third Man)

Reissues The Pile Driver; Hit Him Again; The Rival Suitors

Her Friend the Bandit
4 June: (1000 ft): Keystone
Producer Mack Sennett *Directors* Mabel Normand, Charles Chaplin
Cast Mabel Normand (Miss De Rock), Charles Chaplin (The Bandit), Charles Murray (Count De Beans)
Reissues Mabel's Flirtation; The Thief Catcher

The Knockout
11 June: (1960 ft): Keystone
Producer Mack Sennett *Director* Charles Avery
Cast Roscoe Arbuckle (Fatty), Minta Durfee (Girl), Edgar Kennedy (Cyclone Flynn), Charles Chaplin (Referee), Mack Swain (Spectator), Alice Howell (Spectator), Al StJohn, Hank Mann (Boxer), Mack Sennett (Spectator), George Summerville, Charles Parrott (Cop), Joe Bordeaux (Cop), Edward Cline (Cop)
Reissues Counted Out; The Pugilist

Mabel's Busy Day
13 June: (998 ft): Keystone
Producer Mack Sennett *Directors* Mabel Normand, Charles Chaplin
Cast Mabel Normand (Mabel), Charles Chaplin (The Knut), Chester Conklin (Sergeant), Harry McCoy, Billie Bennett (Girl), George Summerville (Cop), Wallace MacDonald
Reissues Hot Dogs; Love and Lunch; Charlie and the Sausages; Hot Dog Charlie

Mabel's Married Life
20 June: (1015 ft): Keystone
Producer Mack Sennett *Directors* Mabel Normand, Charles Chaplin
Cast Mabel Normand (Mabel), Charles Chaplin (Husband), Mack Swain (Sportsman), Charles Murray (Man at Bar), Harry McCoy (Man at Bar), Alice Howell (Sportsman's Wife), Hank Mann (Friend), Alice Davenport (Neighbour), Al StJohn (Delivery Man), Wallace MacDonald (Delivery Man)
Reissues The Square Head; When You're Married

Laughing Gas
9 July: (1020 ft): Keystone
Producer Mack Sennett *Director* Charles Chaplin
Story/Screenplay Charles Chaplin
Cast Charles Chaplin (Assistant), Fritz Schade (Dr Pain), Alice Howell (Mrs Pain), Mack Swain (Bystander), George Summerville (Patient), Joseph Swickard (Patient), Edward Sutherland (Assistant)
Reissues Tuning His Ivories; The Dentist; Down and Out; Laffing Gas

The Property Man
1 August: (2118 ft): Keystone
Producer Mack Sennett *Director* Charles Chaplin
Story/Screenplay Charles Chaplin
Cast Charles Chaplin (Props), Fritz Schade (Garlico), Phyllis Allen (Hamlena Fat), Alice Davenport (Actress), Charles Bennett (Actor), Mack Sennett (Man in Audience), Harry McCoy, Lee Morris
Reissues Getting His Goat; The Roustabout; Props; Charlie on the Boards

The Face on the Bar-room Floor
10 August: (1020 ft): Keystone
Producer Mack Sennett *Director* Charles Chaplin
Story/Screenplay Charles Chaplin *From the Poem by* Hugh Antoine D'Arcy
Cast Charles Chaplin (Artist), Cecile Arnold (Madeleine), Fritz Schade (Client), Chester Conklin (Man), Vivian Edward (Girl), Harry McCoy (Drinker)
Reissue The Ham Artist

Recreation
13 August: (462 ft): Keystone
Producer Mack Sennett *Director* Charles Chaplin
Story/Screenplay Charles Chaplin
Cast Charles Chaplin (Tramp), Alice Davenport (Woman), Rhea Mitchell (Girl)
Reissue Spring Fever

The Masquerader
27 August: (1030 ft): Keystone
Producer Mack Sennett *Director* Charles Chaplin
Story/Screenplay Charles Chaplin
Cast Charles Chaplin (Himself), Roscoe Arbuckle (Himself), Charles Murray (Director), Chester Conklin (Himself), Fritz Schade (Villain), Minta Durfee (Heroine), Cecile Arnold (Actress), Vivian Edwards (Actress), Harry McCoy (Actor), Charles Parrott (Actor)
Reissues Putting One Over; The Female Impersonator; The Picnic; The Perfumed Lady

His New Profession
31 August: (1015 ft): Keystone
Producer Mack Sennett *Director* Charles Chaplin
Story/Screenplay Charles Chaplin
Cast Charles Chaplin (Charlie), Minta Durfee (Girl), Fritz Schade (Uncle), Charles Parrott (Nephew), Cecile Arnold (Girl), Harry McCoy (Cop)
Reissues The Good-for-nothing; Helping Himself

The Rounders
5 September: (1010 ft): Keystone
Producer Mack Sennett *Director* Charles Chaplin
Story/Screenplay Charles Chaplin
Cast Charles Chaplin (Mr Full), Roscoe Arbuckle (Mr Fuller), Phyllis Allen (Mrs Full), Minta Durfee (Mrs Fuller), Fritz Schade (Diner), Al StJohn (Bellhop), Charles Parrott (Diner), Wallace MacDonald (Diner)
Reissues Revelry; Two of a Kind; Oh What a Night; Going Down

The New Janitor
24 September: (1020 ft): Keystone
Producer Mack Sennett *Director* Charles Chaplin
Story/Screenplay Charles Chaplin
Cast Charles Chaplin (Janitor), Fritz Schade (President), Minta Durfee (Stenographer), Jack Dillon (Clerk), Al StJohn (Liftboy)
Reissues The New Porter; The Blundering Boob

Those Love Pangs
10 October: (1010 ft): Keystone
Producer Mack Sennett *Director* Charles Chaplin
Story/Screenplay Charles Chaplin
Cast Charles Chaplin (The Flirt), Chester Conklin (Rival), Cecile Arnold (Girl), Vivian Edwards (Girl), Edgar Kennedy (Man), Norma Nichols (Landlady), Harry McCoy (Cop)
Reissues The Rival Mashers; Busted Hearts; Oh You Girls

Dough and Dynamite
26 October: (2000 ft): Keystone
Producer Mack Sennett *Directors* Charles Chaplin, Mack Sennett *Story/Screenplay* Charles Chaplin
Cast Charles Chaplin (Pierre), Chester Conklin (Jacques), Fritz Schade (M La Vie), Cecile Arnold (Waitress), Vivian Edwards (Waitress), Phyllis Allen (Customer), Edgar Kennedy (Baker), Charles Parrott (Baker), George Summerville (Baker), Norma Nichols (Mme La Vie), Wallace MacDonald (Baker), Jack Dillon (Customer)
Reissues Doughnut Designers; The Cook

Gentlemen of Nerve
29 October: (1030 ft): Keystone
Producer Mack Sennett *Director* Charles Chaplin
Story/Screenplay Charles Chaplin
Cast Charles Chaplin (Mr Wow-Wow), Mabel Normand
(Mabel), Mack Swain (Ambrose), Chester Conklin
(Walrus), Phyllis Allen (Wife), Edgar Kennedy (Cop),
Charles Parrott (Spectator), George Summerville
(Spectator), Alice Davenport (Waitress)
Reissues Some Nerve; Charlie at the Races

His Musical Career
7 November: (1025 ft): Keystone
Producer Mack Sennett *Director* Charles Chaplin
Story/Screenplay Charles Chaplin
Cast Charles Chaplin (Tom), Mack Swain (Ambrose),
Fritz Schade (Mr Rich), Alice Howell (Mrs Rich),
Charles Parrott (Manager), Joe Bordeaux (Mr Poor),
Norma Nichols (Mrs Poor)
Reissues The Piano Movers; Musical Tramps; Charlie
as a Piano Mover

His Trysting Place
9 November: (2000 ft): Keystone
Producer Mack Sennett *Director* Charles Chaplin
Story/Screenplay Charles Chaplin
Cast Charles Chaplin (Clarence), Mabel Normand
(Mabel), Mack Swain (Ambrose), Phyllis Allen
(Mrs Ambrose)
Reissues Family House; The Ladies Man; The
Henpecked Spouse; Very Much Married

Tillie's Punctured Romance
14 November: (6000 ft): Keystone
Producer Mack Sennett *Director* Mack Sennett
Screenplay Hampton Del Ruth *From the play* Tillie's
Nightmare by Edgar Smith
Cast Marie Dressler (Tillie Banks), Charles Chaplin
(Charlie), Mabel Normand (Mabel), Mack Swain (John
Banks), Charles Bennett (Douglas Banks), Charles
Murray (Detective), Chester Conklin (Guest), Charles
Parrott (Detective), Edgar Kennedy (Proprietor), Harry
McCoy (Pianist), Minta Durfee (Maid), Phyllis Allen
(Wardress), Alice Davenport (Guest), Alice Howell
(Guest), George Summerville (Cop), Al StJohn (Cop),
Wallace MacDonald (Cop), Hank Mann (Cop), Edward
Sutherland (Cop), Joe Bordeaux (Cop), Gordon Griffith
(Newsboy), Billie Bennett (Girl), G. G. Ligon (Cop),
Rev D Simpson (Himself)
Reissues Marie's Millions; For the Love of Tillie
Reissue with soundtrack 3645 ft
Musical director Edward Kilveni *Editor* Guy
V. Thayer jr *Titles* Mort Greene

Getting Acquainted
5 December: (1025 ft): Keystone
Producer Mack Sennett *Director* Charles Chaplin
Story/Screenplay Charles Chaplin
Cast Charles Chaplin (Mr Sniffles), Mabel Normand
(Mrs Ambrose), Mack Swain (Ambrose), Phyllis Allen
(Mrs Sniffles), Harry McCoy (Cop), Edgar Kennedy
(Turk), Cecile Arnold (Girl)
Reissues A Fair Exchange; Hello Everybody

His Prehistoric Past
7 December: (2000 ft): Keystone
Producer Mack Sennett *Director* Charles Chaplin
Story/Screenplay Charles Chaplin
Cast Charles Chaplin (Weakchin), Mack Swain (King
Lowbrow), Fritz Schade (Cleo), Gene Marsh (Favorite
Wife), Cecile Arnold (Cavegirl), Al StJohn (Caveman)
Reissues A Dream; The Hula Hula Dance

1915

His New Job
1 February: (2000 ft): Essanay
Producer Jesse J. Robbins *Director* Charles Chaplin
Story/Screenplay Charles Chaplin *Photography* Rolland
Totheroh
Cast Charles Chaplin (Himself), Ben Turpin (Himself),
Charlotte Mineau (Actress), Charles Insley (Director),
Leo White (Actor), Frank J. Coleman (Manager), Gloria
Swanson (Stenographer), Agnes Ayars (Stenographer)
Reissue Charlie's New Job

A Night Out
10 February: (2000 ft): Essanay
Producer Jesse J. Robbins *Director* Charles Chaplin
Story/Screenplay Charles Chaplin *Photography* Rolland
Totheroh, Harry Ensign *Assistant Director* Ernest Van
Pelt
Cast Charles Chaplin (Drunk), Ben Turpin (Drunk),
Leo White (Count), Bud Jamison (Waiter), Edna
Purviance (Wife), Fred Goodwins (Man)
Reissues Charlie's Night Out; Charlie's Drunken Daze;
His Night Out

The Champion
5 March: (2000 ft): Essanay
Producer Jesse J. Robbins *Director* Charles Chaplin
Story/Screenplay Charles Chaplin *Photography* Rolland
Totheroh, Harry Ensign *Assistant Director* Ernest Van
Pelt
Cast Charles Chaplin (Tramp), Edna Purviance (Girl),
Bud Jamison (Champion), Leo White (Count), Billy
Armstrong (Sparring Partner), Paddy McGuire
(Sparring Partner), Carl Stockdale (Sparring Partner),
Lloyd Bacon (Spike Dugan), Ben Turpin (Salesman),
G. M. Anderson (Spectator)
Reissues Champion Charlie; Charlie the Champion

In The Park
12 March: (1000 ft): Essanay
Producer Jesse J. Robbins *Director* Charles Chaplin
Story/Screenplay Charles Chaplin *Photography* Rolland
Totheroh, Harry Ensign *Assistant Director* Ernest Van
Pelt
Cast Charles Chaplin (Flirt), Edna Purviance
(Nursemaid), Leo White (Count), Lloyd Bacon
(Tramp), Bud Jamison (Boyfriend), Billy Armstrong
(Man), Margie Reiger (Girl), Ernest Van Pelt (Cop)
Reissues Charlie in the Park; Charlie on the Spree

A Jitney Elopement
23 March: (2000 ft): Essanay
Producer Jesse J. Robbins *Director* Charles Chaplin
Story/Screenplay Charles Chaplin *Photography* Rolland
Totheroh, Harry Ensign *Assistant Director* Ernest Van
Pelt
Cast Charles Chaplin (Tramp), Edna Purviance (Girl),
Leo White (Count De Haha), Fred Goodwins (Father),
Paddy McGuire (Old Servant), Lloyd Bacon (Footman),
Bud Jamison (Cop), Ernest Van Pelt (Cop)
Reissues Charlie's Elopement; Married in Haste

The Tramp
7 April: (2000 ft): Essanay
Producer Jesse J. Robbins *Director* Charles Chaplin
Story/Screenplay Charles Chaplin *Photography* Rolland
Totheroh, Harry Ensign *Assistant Director* Ernest Van
Pelt
Cast Charles Chaplin (Tramp), Edna Purviance (Girl),
Leo White (Tramp), Fred Goodwins (Farmer), Bud
Jamison (Tramp), Lloyd Bacon (Sweetheart), Paddy
McGuire (Farmhand), Ernest Van Pelt (Tramp), Billy
Armstrong (Poet)

Reissues Charlie the Tramp; Charlie on the Farm; Charlie the Hobo

By The Sea
26 April: (1000 ft): Essanay
Producer Jesse J. Robbins *Director* Charles Chaplin
Story/Screenplay Charles Chaplin *Photography* Rolland Totheroh, Harry Ensign *Assistant Director* Ernest Van Pelt
Cast Charles Chaplin (Man), Edna Purviance (Girl), Billy Armstrong (Other Man), Bud Jamison (Dandy), Margie Reiger (Girl)
Reissues Charlie by the Sea; Charlie's Day Out

His Regeneration
3 May: (963 ft): Essanay
Producer G. M. Anderson
Cast G. M. Anderson, Lee Willard, Marguerite Clayton, Hazel Applegate, Charles Chaplin

Work
2 June: (2000 ft): Essanay
Producer Jesse J. Robbins *Director* Charles Chaplin
Story/Screenplay Charles Chaplin *Photography* Rolland Totheroh, Harry Ensign *Assistant Director* Ernest Van Pelt *Scenic Artist* E. T. Mazy
Cast Charles Chaplin (Assistant), Edna Purviance (Maid), Charles Insley (Paperhanger), Billy Armstrong (Husband), Marta Golden (Wife), Leo White (Lover), Paddy McGuire (Hod-carrier)
Reissues Charlie the Decorator; The Paperhanger; Charlie at Work

A Woman
7 July: (2000 ft): Essanay
Producer Jesse J. Robbins *Director* Charles Chaplin
Story/Screenplay Charles Chaplin *Photography* Rolland Totheroh, Harry Ensign *Assistant Director* Ernest Van Pelt *Scenic Artist* E. T. Mazy
Cast Charles Chaplin (Tramp), Edna Purviance (Girl), Charles Insley (Father), Marta Golden (Mother), Billy Armstrong (Suitor), Margie Reiger (Flirt), Leo White (Gentleman)
Reissues The Perfect Lady; Charlie the Perfect Lady

The Bank
9 August: (2000 ft): Essanay
Producer Jesse J. Robbins *Director* Charles Chaplin
Story/Screenplay Charles Chaplin *Photography* Rolland Totheroh, Harry Ensign *Assistant Director* Ernest Van Pelt *Scenic Artist* E. T. Mazy
Cast Charles Chaplin (Charlie the Janitor), Edna Purviance (Edna), Carl Stockdale (Charlie the Cashier), Billy Armstrong (Janitor), Charles Insley (Manager), John Rand (Salesman), Fred Goodwins (Thief), Frank J. Coleman (Thief), Wesley Ruggles (Thief), Paddy McGuire, Lloyd Bacon
Reissues Charlie at the Bank; Charlie in the Bank; Charlie, Detective

Shanghaied
27 September: (2000 ft): Essanay
Producer Jesse J. Robbins *Director* Charles Chaplin
Story/Screenplay Charles Chaplin *Photography* Rolland Totheroh, Harry Ensign *Assistant Director* Ernest Van Pelt *Scenic Artist* E. T. Mazy
Cast Charles Chaplin (Tramp), Edna Purviance (Edna), Wesley Ruggles (Owner), John Rand (Captain), Bud Jamison (Mate), Lawrence A. Bowes (Cook), Billy Armstrong (Seaman), Paddy McGuire (Seaman), Leo White (Seaman), Fred Goodwins (Seaman)
Reissues Charlie Shanghaied; Charlie the Sailor; Charlie on the Ocean

A Night in the Show
2 November: (2000 ft): Essanay
Producer Jesse J. Robbins *Director* Charles Chaplin
Story/Screenplay Charles Chaplin *Photography* Rolland Totheroh *Assistant Director* Ernest Van Pelt *Scenic Artist* E. T. Mazy
Cast Charles Chaplin (Mr Pest/Mr Rowdy), Edna Purviance (Lady), Leo White (Count/Prof. Nix), John Rand (Conductor), Bud Jamison (Dot), James T. Kelly (Dash), Dee Lampton (Fat Boy), May White (La Belle Wienerwurst), Paddy McGuire (Trombonist), Fred Goodwins (Tuba Player), Carrie Clarke Ward (Woman)
Reissue Charlie at the Show

Charlie Chaplin's Burlesque on Carmen
December – 3 April 1916: (4000 ft): Essanay
Producer Jesse J. Robbins *Director* Charles Chaplin
Screenplay Charles Chaplin *From the story by* Prosper Merimee *and the opera by* H. Meilhac, L. Halevy, Georges Bizet *Photography* Rolland Totheroh *Assistant Director* Ernest Van Pelt *Scenic Artist* E. T. Mazy
Cast Charles Chaplin (Darn Hosiery), Edna Purviance (Carmen), Ben Turpin (Don Remendado), Leo White (Morales), John Rand (Escamillo), Jack Henderson (Lilias Pasta), May White (Frasquita), Bud Jamison (Soldier), Wesley Ruggles (Tramp), Lawrence A. Bowes, Frank J. Coleman

1916

Police
27 March: (2000 ft): Essanay
Producer Jesse J. Robbins *Director* Charles Chaplin
Story Charles Chaplin, Vincent Bryan *Screenplay* Charles Chaplin *Photography* Rolland Totheroh *Assistant Director* Ernest Van Pelt *Scenic Artist* E. T. Mazy
Cast Charles Chaplin (Convict 999), Edna Purviance (Girl), Wesley Ruggles (Crook), Billy Armstrong (Crook), John Rand (Cop), Leo White (Lodging House Keeper/Vendor/Cop), James T. Kelley (Drunk/Tramp), Fred Goodwins (Cop/Pastor), Bud Jamison (Cop), Frank J. Coleman (Cop)
Reissues Charlie in the Police; Charlie the Burglar

The Floorwalker
15 May: (1734 ft): Lone Star-Mutual *Producer/Director* Charles Chaplin *Story* Charles Chaplin, Vincent Bryan *Screenplay* Charles Chaplin *Photography* William C. Foster, Rolland Totheroh *Scenic Artist* E. T. Mazy
Cast Charles Chaplin (The Floorwalker), Edna Purviance (Secretary), Eric Campbell (George Brush), Lloyd Bacon (Assistant), Albert Austin (Clerk), Leo White (Count), Charlotte Mineau (Detective), Tom Nelson (Detective), Henry Bergman (Old Man), James T. Kelley (Liftboy), Bud Jamison, Stanley Sanford, Frank J. Coleman
Reissue Shop!

The Fireman
12 June: (1921 ft): Lone Star-Mutual
Producer/Director Charles Chaplin *Story* Charles Chaplin, Vincent Bryan *Screenplay* Charles Chaplin *Photography* William C. Foster, Rolland Totheroh *Scenic Artist* E. T. Mazy
Cast Charles Chaplin (The Fireman), Edna Purviance (Edna), Eric Campbell (Captain), Lloyd Bacon (Father), Leo White (Householder), John Rand (Fireman), Albert Austin (Fireman), James T. Kelley (Fireman), Frank J. Coleman (Fireman), Charlotte Mineau (Mother)
Reissues A Gallant Fireman; The Fiery Circle

The Vagabond
10 July: (1956 ft): Lone Star-Mutual
Producer/Director Charles Chaplin *Story* Charles

Chaplin, Vincent Bryan *Screenplay* Charles Chaplin
Photography William C. Foster, Rolland Totheroh
Cast Charles Chaplin (The Vagabond), Edna Purviance
(Girl), Eric Campbell (Gypsy Chief), Leo White (Gypsy
Hag/Jew), Lloyd Bacon (Artist), Charlotte Mineau
(Mother), Phyllis Allen (Woman), John Rand
(Trumpeter), Albert Austin (Trombonist), James T.
Kelley (Bandsman), Frank J. Coleman (Bandsman)
Reissue Gipsy Life

One A.M.
7 August: (2000 ft): Lone Star-Mutual
Producer/Director Charles Chaplin *Story/Screenplay*
Charles Chaplin *Photography* William C. Foster,
Rolland Totheroh *Scenic Artist* E. T. Mazy
Cast Charles Chaplin (The Drunk), Albert Austin
(Taxidriver)
Reissue Solo

The Count
4 September: (2000 ft): Lone Star-Mutual
Producer/Director Charles Chaplin *Story/Screenplay*
Charles Chaplin *Photography* Rolland Totheroh,
William C. Foster
Cast Charles Chaplin (Assistant), Edna Purviance
(Edna Moneybags), Eric Campbell (Buttinsky), Leo
White (Count Broko), Charlotte Mineau (Mrs
Moneybags), James T. Kelley (Butler), Albert Austin
(Guest), Frank J. Coleman (Cop), John Rand (Guest),
May White (Ima Pipp), Stanley Sanford (Guest), Leota
Bryan (Girl), Eva Thatcher (Flirtitia Doughbelle),
Loyal Underwood (Small Man)
Reissue Almost a Gentleman

The Pawn Shop
2 October: (1940 ft): Lone Star-Mutual
Producer/Director Charles Chaplin *Story/Screenplay*
Charles Chaplin *Photography* Rolland Totheroh,
William C. Foster
Cast Charles Chaplin (Assistant), Edna Purviance
(Daughter), Henry Bergman (Pawnbroker), John Rand
(Clerk), Eric Campbell (Thief), Albert Austin
(Customer), Frank J. Coleman (Cop), James T. Kelley
(Customer)
Reissues High and Low Finance; At the Sign of the
Dollar

Behind the Screen
13 November: (1796 ft): Lone Star-Mutual
Producer/Director Charles Chaplin *Story/Screenplay*
Charles Chaplin *Photography* Rolland Totheroh,
William C. Foster
Cast Charles Chaplin (David), Edna Purviance
(Country Girl), Eric Campbell (Goliath), Henry
Bergman (Director), Lloyd Bacon (Director), Albert
Austin (Stage Hand), Frank J. Coleman (Assistant
Director), Charlotte Mineau (Actress), John Rand
(Stage Hand), James T. Kelley (Cameraman)
Reissues The Pride of Hollywood; Los Fallen Angeles

The Rink
4 December: (1881 ft): Lone Star-Mutual
Producer/Director Charles Chaplin
Story/Screenplay Charles Chaplin *Photography* Rolland
Totheroh, William C. Foster
Cast Charles Chaplin (Waiter), Edna Purviance (Edna
Loneleigh), Eric Campbell (Mr Stout), Henry Bergman
(Mrs Stout), Frank J. Coleman (Mr Loneleigh),
Charlotte Mineau (Friend), Albert Austin
(Cook/Skater), James T. Kelley (Cook), John Rand
(Fritz), Lloyd Bacon (Customer)
Reissues Rolling Around; Waiter!

1917

Easy Street
22 January: (1757 ft): Lone Star-Mutual
Producer/Director Charles Chaplin *Story/Screenplay*
Charles Chaplin *Photography* Rolland Totheroh,
William C. Foster
Cast Charles Chaplin (Tramp), Edna Purviance
(Missioner), Eric Campbell (Big Eric), Henry Bergman
(Anarchist), Albert Austin (Minister/Cop), James T.
Kelley (Missioner/Cop), John Rand (Tramp/Cop),
Frank J. Coleman (Cop), Leo White (Cop), Charlotte
Mineau (Wife), Lloyd Bacon (Drug Addict), Janet
Miller Sully (Mother), Loyal Underwood (Police
Chief/Father)

The Cure
16 April: (1834 ft): Lone Star-Mutual
Producer/Director Charles Chaplin *Story/Screenplay*
Charles Chaplin *Photography* Rolland Totheroh,
William C. Foster
Cast Charles Chaplin (Drunk), Edna Purviance (Girl),
Eric Campbell (Patient), Henry Bergman (Masseur),
John Rand (Attendant), Albert Austin (Attendant),
Frank J. Coleman (Proprietor), James T. Kelley
(Bellhop), Leota Bryan (Nurse), Janet Miller Sully
(Woman), Loyal Underwood (Patient), Tom Wood
(Patient)
Reissue The Water Cure

The Immigrant
17 June: (1809 ft): Lone Star-Mutual
Producer/Director Charles Chaplin *Story/Screenplay*
Charles Chaplin *Photography* Rolland Totheroh,
William C. Foster
Cast Charles Chaplin (Immigrant), Edna Purviance
(Girl), Eric Campbell (Head Waiter), Kitty Bradbury
(Mother), Albert Austin (Immigrant/Diner), Henry
Bergman (Woman/Artist), James T. Kelley
(Tramp/Immigrant), Frank J. Coleman
(Proprietor/Official), Stanley Sanford (Gambler), John
Rand (Customer), Loyal Underwood (Immigrant)
Reissues The New World; A Modern Columbus; Hello
U.S.A.

The Adventurer
22 October: (1845 ft): Lone Star-Mutual
Producer/Director Charles Chaplin *Story/Screenplay*
Charles Chaplin *Photography* Rolland Totheroh,
William C. Foster
Cast Charles Chaplin (Convict), Edna Purviance (Girl),
Eric Campbell (Suitor), Henry Bergman
(Father/Workman), Marta Golden (Mother), Albert
Austin (Butler), Frank J. Coleman (Guard), James T.
Kelley (Old Man), Phyllis Allen (Governess), Toraichi
Kono (Chauffeur), John Rand (Guest), May White
(Lady), Loyal Underwood (Guest), Janet Miller Sully
(Marie), Monta Bell (Man)

1918

A Dog's Life
12 April: (2674 ft): Chaplin-First National
Producer/Director Charles Chaplin *Story/Screenplay*
Charles Chaplin *Photography* Rolland Totheroh
Assistant Director Charles Reisner
Cast Charles Chaplin (Tramp), Edna Purviance
(Singer), Sydney Chaplin (Proprietor), Tom Wilson
(Cop), Albert Austin (Thief), Henry Bergman
(Tramp/Woman), James T. Kelley (Thief), Charles
Reisner (Clerk), Billy White (Cafe Owner), Janet Miller
Sully (Singer), Bud Jamison (Client), Loyal Underwood
(Client), Park Jones (Waiter), Scraps (The Dog)

Triple Trouble
23 July: (2000 ft): Essanay
Producer Jesse J. Robbins *Directors* Charles Chaplin, Leo White *Story/Screenplay* Charles Chaplin, Leo White *Photography* Rolland Totheroh *Assistant Director* Ernest Van Pelt
Cast Charles Chaplin (Janitor), Edna Purviance (Maid), Leo White (Count), Billy Armstrong (Cook/Thief), James T. Kelley (Singer), Bud Jamison (Tramp), Wesley Ruggles (Crook), Albert Austin (Man)
Reissue Charlie's Triple Trouble

Shoulder Arms
2 October: (3142 ft): Chaplin-First National
Producer/Director Charles Chaplin *Story/Screenplay* Charles Chaplin *Photography* Rolland Totheroh *Assistant Director* Charles Reisner
Cast Charles Chaplin (Rookie), Edna Purviance (French Girl), Sydney Chaplin (Kaiser Wilhelm/Soldier), Henry Bergman (Hindenberg/Bartender/Officer), Jack Wilson (Crown Prince/Soldier), Albert Austin (Officer/Kaiser's driver/Rookie), Tom Wilson (Sergeant), John Rand (Soldier), Loyal Underwood (Captain), Park Jones (Soldier)

Charles Chaplin in a Liberty Loan Appeal
4 October: (500 ft): Chaplin/Liberty Loan Committee
Producer/Director Charles Chaplin *Story/Screenplay* Charles Chaplin *Photography* Rolland Totheroh
Cast Charles Chaplin (Charlie), Sydney Chaplin (The Kaiser), Edna Purviance, Albert Austin
Retitled The Bond

1919

Sunnyside
4 June: (2769 ft): Chaplin-First National
Producer/Director Charles Chaplin *Story/Screenplay* Charles Chaplin *Photography* Rolland Totheroh
Cast Charles Chaplin (Handyman), Edna Purviance (Girl), Tom Wilson (Boss), Henry Bergman (Father), Albert Austin (Slicker), Loyal Underwood (Old Man), Park Jones (Fat Man), Tom Wood (Peasant), Tom Terriss (City Man)

A Day's Pleasure
26 November: (1714 ft): Chaplin-First National
Producer/Director Charles Chaplin *Story/Screenplay* Charles Chaplin *Photography* Rolland Totheroh
Cast Charles Chaplin (Father), Edna Purviance (Mother), Tom Wilson (Cop), Sydney Chaplin (Father), Henry Bergman (Captain), Babe London (Fat Girl), Albert Austin (Trombonist), Loyal Underwood (Musician), Raymond Lee (Boy), Jackie Coogan (Boy)

1921

The Kid
17 January: (5300 ft): Chaplin-First National
Producer/Director Charles Chaplin *Story/Screenplay* Charles Chaplin *Photography* Rolland Totheroh *Associate Director* Charles Reisner
Cast Charles Chaplin (Tramp), Edna Purviance (Woman), Jackie Coogan (Kid), Carl Miller (Artist), Tom Wilson (Cop), Charles Reisner (Bully), Henry Bergman (Proprietor), Albert Austin (Crook), Phyllis Allen (Woman), Nellie Bly Baker (Neighbour), Jack Coogan (Man), Monta Bell (Man), Raymond Lee (Boy), Lolita McMurray (Angel)

The Nut
3 March: (6000 ft): Fairbanks-United Artists
Producer Douglas Fairbanks *Director* Theodore Reed *Story* Kenneth Davenport *Screenplay* William Parker,

Lotta Woods *Photography* William McGann
Cast Douglas Fairbanks (Charlie Jackson), Marguerite de la Motte (Estrelle Wynn), William Lowery (Philip Feeney), Gerald Pring (Gentleman George), Morris Hughes (Perrelius Vanderbrook), Barbara La Marr (Claudine Dupree), Charles Chaplin (Himself)

The Idle Class
6 September: (1916 ft): Chaplin-First National
Producer/Director Charles Chaplin *Story/Screenplay* Charles Chaplin *Photography* Rolland Totheroh
Cast Charles Chaplin (Tramp/Husband), Edna Purviance (Wife), Mack Swain (Father), Henry Bergman (Tramp/Cop), Rex Storey (Robber/Guest), John Rand (Tramp/Guest), Allan Garcia (Golfer/Guest), Loyal Underwood (Guest), Lillian McMurray (Maid), Lita Grey (Maid)

1922

Pay Day
13 March: (1892 ft): Chaplin-First National
Producer/Director Charles Chaplin *Story/Screenplay* Charles Chaplin *Photography* Rolland Totheroh
Cast Charles Chaplin (Worker), Edna Purviance (Daughter), Mack Swain (Foreman), Phyllis Allen (Wife), Sydney Chaplin (Friend/Proprietor), Henry Bergman (Drinker), Allan Garcia (Drinker), Albert Austin (Workman), John Rand (Workman), Loyal Underwood (Workman)

Nice and Friendly
Producer/Director Charles Chaplin *Story/Screenplay* Charles Chaplin
Cast Charles Chaplin, Lord Louis Mountbatten, Lady Edwina Mountbatten, Jackie Coogan, Colonel Robert M. Thompson, Frederick Neilson, Eulalie Neilson

1923

The Pilgrim
24 January: (4300 ft): Chaplin-First National
Producer/Director Charles Chaplin *Story/Screenplay* Charles Chaplin *Photography* Rolland Totheroh *Associate Director* Charles Reisner
Cast Charles Chaplin (Pilgrim), Edna Purviance (Edna Brown), Mack Swain (Deacon), Kitty Bradbury (Mrs Brown), Dinky Dean Reisner (Boy), Sydney Chaplin (Father), Mai Wells (Mother), Charles Reisner (Thief), Loyal Underwood (Elder), Tom Murray (Sheriff), Monta Bell (Policeman), Henry Bergman (Traveller), Raymond Lee (Pastor), Edith Bostwick (Lady), Florence Latimer (Lady), Phyllis Allen (Lady)

Souls for Sale
27 March: (7864 ft): Goldwyn
Producer/Director Rupert Hughes *Screenplay* Rupert Hughes *From the novel by* Rupert Hughes *Photography* John Mescall
Cast Eleanor Boardman (Remember Steddon), Mae Busch (Robina Teele), Barbara LaMarr (Leva Lemaire), Richard Dix (Frank Claymore), Frank Mayo (Tom Holby), Lew Cody (Owen Scudder), Arthur Hoyt (Jimmy Leland), David Imboden (Caxton), Roy Atwell (Arthur Terry), William Orlamond (Lord Fryingham), Forrest Robinson (John Steddon), Edith Yorke (Mrs Steddon), Dale Fuller (Abigail Tweedy), Snitz Edwards (Hank Kale), Aileen Pringle (Lady Jane), Eve Southern (Velma Slade), Fred Kelsey (Quinn), Jed Prouty (Magnus), Yale Boss (Prop Man), William Haines (Pinky)
Themselves Hugo Ballin, Mabel Ballin, T. Roy Barnes, Barbara Bedford, Hobart Bosworth, Charles Chaplin, Chester Conklin, William H. Crane, Elliott Dexter, Robert Edeson, Claude Gillingwater, Dagmar

Godowsky, Raymond Griffith, Elaine Hammerstein, Jean Haskell, K.C.B., Alice Lake, Bessie Love, June Mathis, Patsy Ruth Miller, Marshall Neilan, Fred Niblo, Anna Q. Nilsson, Zasu Pitts, John Sainpolis, Milton Sills, Anita Stewart, Erich von Stroheim, Blanche Sweet, Florence Vidor, King Vidor, Johnny Walker, George Walsh, Kathlyn Williams, Claire Windsor

A Woman of Paris
1 October: (7577 ft): Regent-United Artists
Producer/Director Charles Chaplin *Story/Screenplay* Charles Chaplin *Photography* Rolland Totheroh *Cameraman* Jack Wilson *Assistant Director* Edward Sutherland *Literary Editor* Monta Bell *Art Director* Arthur Stibolt *Research* Jean de Limur, Henri d'Abbadie d'Arrast
Cast Edna Purviance (Marie StClair), Adolphe Menjou (Pierre Revel), Carl Miller (Jean Millet), Lydia Knott (Mme Millet), Charles French (M. Millet), Clarence Geldert (M. StClair), Betty Morrissey (Fifi), Malvina Polo (Paulette), Karl Gutman (Conductor), Henry Bergman (Maitre d'hotel), Harry Northrup (Valet), Nellie Bly Baker (Masseuse), Charles Chaplin (Porter)

1925

The Gold Rush
16 August: (8498 ft): Chaplin-United Artists
Producer/Director Charles Chaplin *Story/Screenplay* Charles Chaplin *Photography* Rolland Totheroh *Cameraman* Jack Wilson *Technical Director* Charles D. Hall *Associate Directors* Charles Reisner, Henri d'Abbadie d'Arrast *Production Manager* Alfred Reeves
Cast Charles Chaplin (The Lone Prospector), Georgia Hale (Georgia), Mack Swain (Big Jim McKay), Tom Murray (Black Larsen), Malcolm Waite (Jack Cameron), Henry Bergman (Hank Curtis), Betty Morrissey (Betty), John Rand (Prospector), Albert Austin (Prospector), Heinie Conklin (Prospector), Allan Garcia (Prospector), Tom Wood (Prospector)
Reissue with soundtrack 18 April 1942 (72 mins)
Music Charles Chaplin *Narrator* Charles Chaplin

1926

A Woman of the Sea
(length unknown): Chaplin
Producer Charles Chaplin *Directors* Josef von Sternberg, Charles Chaplin *Story* Charles Chaplin *Screenplay* Josef von Sternberg *Photography* Paul Ivano *Art Director* Charles D. Hall
Cast Edna Purviance (The Woman), Eve Southern, Gayne Whitman

1928

The Circus
6 January: (6700 ft): Chaplin-United Artists
Producer/Director Charles Chaplin *Story/Screenplay* Charles Chaplin *Photography* Rolland Totheroh *Cameramen* Jack Wilson, Mark Marklatt *Assistant Director* Harry Crocker *Art Director* Charles D. Hall *Editor* Charles Chaplin *Laboratory Supervisor* William E. Hinckley
Cast Charles Chaplin (The Tramp), Merna Kennedy (The Equestrienne), Betty Morrissey (The Vanishing Lady), Harry Crocker (Rex), Allan Garcia (Proprietor), Henry Bergman (Merry Clown), Stanley J. Sanford (Ringmaster), George Davis (Magician), John Rand (Property Man), Steve Murphy (Pickpocket), Doc Stone (Boxer), Albert Austin, Heinie Conklin
Reissue with soundtrack 1970 (71 mins)
Music Charles Chaplin *Song* Charles Chaplin *Singer* Charles Chaplin

Show People
20 October: (7453 ft): Metro-Goldwyn-Mayer
Producers Marion Davies, King Vidor *Director* King Vidor *Treatment* Agnes Christine Johnston, Laurence Stallings *Continuity* Wanda Tuchock *Photography* John Arnold *Art Director* Cedric Gibbons *Editor* Hugh Wynn *Song* William Axt, David Mendoza *Costumes* Henrietta Frazer *Titles* Ralph Spence
Cast Marion Davies (Peggy Pepper), William Haines (Billy Boone), Dell Henderson (Col Pepper), Paul Ralli (Andre), Tenen Holtz (Casting Director), Harry Gribbon (Comedy Director), Sidney Bracy (Dramatic Director), Polly Moran (Maid), Albert Conti (Producer)
Themselves Charles Chaplin, Douglas Fairbanks, John Gilbert, Elinor Glyn, Mae Murray

1931

City Lights
1 February: (87 mins): Chaplin-United Artists
Producer/Director Charles Chaplin *Story/Screenplay* Charles Chaplin *Photography* Rolland Totheroh *Cameramen* Gordon Pollock, Mark Marklatt *Assistant Directors* Harry Crocker, Henry Bergman, Albert Austin *Art Director* Charles D. Hall *Music* Charles Chaplin; Padilla (La Violetera) *Music Arranger* Arthur Johnson *Music Director* Alfred Newman *Production Manager* Alfred Reeves
Cast Charles Chaplin (The Tramp), Virginia Cherrill (The Blind Girl), Harry Myers (The Millionaire), Hank Mann (Boxer), Allan Garcia (Butler), Florence Lee (Grandmother), Henry Bergman (Mayor/Janitor), Albert Austin (Sweeper/Crook), John Rand (Tramp), James Donnelly (Foreman), Robert Parrish (Newsboy), Stanhope Wheatcroft (Man in Cafe), Jean Harlow (Guest)

1936

Modern Times
5 February: (85 mins): Chaplin-United Artists
Producer/Director Charles Chaplin *Story/Screenplay* Charles Chaplin *Photography* Rolland Totheroh, Ira Morgan *Assistant Directors* Carter De Haven, Henry Bergman *Art Directors* Charles D. Hall, J. Russell Spencer *Music* Charles Chaplin; Leo Daniderff (Je Cherche Apres Titine) *Music Arrangers* Edward Powell, David Raksin *Music Director* Alfred Newman *Production Managers* Alfred Reeves, Jack Wilson
Cast Charles Chaplin (A Worker), Paulette Goddard (A Gamin), Henry Bergman (Proprietor), Stanley J. Sanford (Big Bill), Chester Conklin (Mechanic), Hank Mann (Burglar), Stanley Blystone (Sheriff Couler), Allan Garcia (President), Dick Alexander (Convict), Cecil Reynolds (Chaplain), Myra McKinney (Chaplain's Wife), Lloyd Ingraham (Governor), Louis Natheaux (Addict), Heinie Conklin (Workman), Frank Moran (Convict), Murdoch McQuarrie, Wilfred Lucas, Edward le Saint, Fred Maltesta, Sam Stein, Juana Sutton, Ted Oliver, Edward Kimball, John Rand, Walter James

1940

The Great Dictator
15 October: (126 mins): Chaplin-United Artists
Producer/Director Charles Chaplin *Story/Screenplay* Charles Chaplin *Photography* Rolland Totheroh, Karl Struss *Assistant Directors* Daniel James, Wheeler Dryden, Robert Meltzer *Coordinator* Henry Bergman *Art Director* J. Russell Spencer *Editor* Willard Nico *Music* Charles Chaplin; Wagner, Brahms *Music Director* Meredith Willson *Sound* Percy Townsend, Glenn Rominger
Cast Charles Chaplin (Adenoid Hynkel/The Barber),

Paulette Goddard (Hannah), Jack Oakie (Benzino Napaloni), Henry Daniell (Garbitsch), Reginald Gardiner (Schultz), Billy Gilbert (Herring), Maurice Moskovich (Mr Jaeckel), Emma Dunn (Mrs Jaeckel), Bernard Gorcey (Mr Mann), Paul Weigel (Mr Agar), Grace Hayle (Madame Napaloni), Carter De Haven (Ambassador), Chester Conklin (Customer), Eddie Gribbon (Stormtrooper), Hank Mann (Stormtrooper), Leo White (Barber), Lucien Prival (Officer), Richard Alexander (Stormtrooper), Esther Michelson, Florence Wright, Robert O. David, Eddie Dunn, Peter Lynn Hayes, Nita Pike, Harry Semels, Jack Perrin, Pat Flaherty

1947

Monsieur Verdoux
11 April: (122 mins): Chaplin-United Artists
Producer/Director Charles Chaplin *Story/Screenplay* Charles Chaplin *From an idea by* Orson Welles *Photography* Rolland Totheroh, Curt Courant, Wallace Chewing *Associate Director* Robert Florey, *Assistant Directors* Rex Bailey, Wheeler Dryden *Art Director* John Beckman *Editor* Willard Nico *Music* Charles Chaplin *Music Director* Rudolph Schrager *Sound* James T. Corrigan *Costumes* Drew Tetrick *Narrator* Charles Chaplin
Cast Charles Chaplin (Henri Verdoux), Martha Raye (Annabella Bonheur), Isobel Elsom (Marie Grosnay), Marilyn Nash (The Girl), Robert Lewis (Maurice Bottello), Mady Correll (Mona Verdoux), Allison Rodell (Peter Verdoux), Audrey Betz (Martha Bottello), Ada-May (Annette), Marjorie Bennett (Maid), Helene Heigh (Yvonne), Margaret Hoffman (Lydia Floray), Irving Bacon (Pierre Couvais), Edwin Mills (Jean Couvais), Virginia Brissac (Carlotta Couvais), Almira Sessions (Lena Couvais), Eula Morgan (Phoebe Couvais), Bernard J. Nedell (Prefect), Charles Evans (Detective Morron), Arthur Hohl (Estate Agent), John Harmon (Joe Darwin), Vera Marshe (Mrs Darwin), William Frawley (Jean la Salle), Fritz Lieber (Priest), Barbara Slater (Florist), Fred Karno jr (Mr Karno), Barry Norton (Guest), Pierre Watkin (Official), Cyril Delevanti (Postman), Charles Wagenheim (Friend), Addison Richards (Manager), James Craven (Friend), Franklin Farnum (Victim), Herb Vigran (Reporter), Boyd Irwin (Official), Paul Newland (Guest), Joseph Crehan (Broker), Wheaton Chambers (Druggist), Frank Reicher (Doctor), Wheeler Dryden (Salesman), Edna Purviance (Extra), Christine Ell, Lois Conklin, Tom Wilson, Phillips Smalley

1952

Limelight
23 October: (143 mins): Celebrated-United Artists
Producer/Director Charles Chaplin *Story/Screenplay* Charles Chaplin *Associate Director* Robert Aldrich *Assistant Producers* Jerome Epstein, Wheeler Dryden *Photography* Karl Struss *Photographic Consultant* Rolland Totheroh *Art Director* Eugene Lourie *Editor* Joseph Engel *Music* Charles Chaplin *Songs* Charles Chaplin, Ray Rasch *Choreography* Charles Chaplin, Andre Eglevsky, Melissa Hayden
Cast Charles Chaplin (Calvero), Claire Bloom (Terry – Thereza), Nigel Bruce (Postant), Buster Keaton (Partner), Sydney Chaplin (Neville), Norman Lloyd (Bodalink), Andre Eglevsky (Harlequin), Melissa Hayden (Columbine), Marjorie Bennett (Mrs Alsop), Wheeler Dryden (Doctor/Clown), Barry Bernard (John Redfern), Leonard Mudie (Doctor), Snub Pollard (Musician), Charles Chaplin jr (Clown), Geraldine Chaplin (Child), Michael Chaplin (Child), Josephine Chaplin (Child), Edna Purviance (Woman), Loyal

Underwood, Stapleton Kent, Mollie Blessing, Julian Ludwig

1957

A King in New York
12 September: (109 mins): Attica-Archway
Producer/Director Charles Chaplin *Story/Screenplay* Charles Chaplin *Photography* Georges Perinal *Art Director* Allan Harris *Editor* John Seabourne *Music* Charles Chaplin *Sound* Spencer Reeves
Cast Charles Chaplin (King Shahdov), Dawn Addams (Ann Kay), Oliver Johnston (Jaume), Maxine Audley (Queen Irene), Jerry Desmonde (Prime Minister), Michael Chaplin (Rupert McAbee), Harry Green (Lawyer Green), Phil Brown (Headmaster), John McLaren (McAbee Sr), Alan Gifford (School Superintendent), Shani Wallis (Singer), Joy Nichols (Singer), Joan Ingram (Mona Cromwell), Sidney James (Johnson), Robert Arden (Liftboy), Nicholas Tannar (Butler), Lauri Lupino Lane (Comedian), George Truzzi (Comedian), George Woodbridge, Macdonald Parke

1959

The Chaplin Revue
25 September: (117 mins): Roy-United Artists
Producer/Director Charles Chaplin *Screenplay* Charles Chaplin *Music* Charles Chaplin *Song* Charles Chaplin (Bound for Texas) *Narrator* Charles Chaplin *Singer* Matt Munro
Compiled from A Dog's Life; Shoulder Arms; The Pilgrim

1966

A Countess from Hong Kong
November: (120 mins): Universal
Producer Jerome Epstein *Director* Charles Chaplin *Story/Screenplay* Charles Chaplin *Photography* Arthur Ibbetson *Production Supervisor* Denis Johnson *Production Designer* Don Ashton *Art Director* Robert Cartwright *Set Decorator* Vernon Dixon *Editor* Gordon Hales *Assistant Director* Jack Causey *Music* Charles Chaplin *Music Director* Lambert Williamson *Music Associate* Eric James *Sound* Michael Hopkins *Sound Recording* Bill Daniels, Ken Barker *Titles* Gordon Shadrick *Colour* Technicolor *Process* Cinemascope
Cast Marlon Brando (Ogden Mears), Sophia Loren (Countess Natascha Alexandroff), Sydney Chaplin (Harvey Crothers), Tippi Hedren (Martha Mears), Patrick Cargill (Hudson), Margaret Rutherford (Miss Gaulswallow), Michael Medwin (John Felix), Oliver Johnston (Clark), John Paul (Captain), Angela Scoular (Society Girl), Peter Bartlett (Steward), Bill Nagy (Crawford), Dilys Laye (Saleswoman), Angela Pringle (Baroness), Jenny Bridges (Countess), Arthur Gross (Immigration Officer), Balbina (Maid), Anthony Chin (Hawaiian), Jose Sukhum Boonlve (Hawaiian), Geraldine Chaplin (Girl at Dance), Janine Hill (Girl at Dance), Burnell Tucker (Receptionist), Leonard Trolley (Purser), Len Lowe (Electrician), Francis Dux (Headwaiter), Cecil Cheng (Taxidriver), Ronald Rubin (Sailor), Michael Spice (Sailor), Ray Marlowe (Sailor), Josephine Chaplin (Young Girl), Victoria Chaplin (Young Girl), Kevin Manser (Photographer), Marianne Stone (Reporter), Lew Luton (Reporter), Larry Cross (Reporter), Bill Edwards (Reporter), Drew Russell (Reporter), John Sterland (Reporter), Paul Carson (Reporter), Paul Tamarin (Reporter), Carol Cleveland (Nurse), Charles Chaplin (An Old Steward)

His Musical Career

Musical Compositions
1916 There's Always One You Can't Forget
1916 Oh! That 'Cello
1916 The Peace Patrol
1921 *The Kid*: The Kid; Blue Eyes; Morning Promenade
1921 *The Idle Class*: Foxtrot; South American
1925 Sing a Song
1925 With You Dear in Bombay
1931 *City Lights*
1936 *Modern Times*: The Factory Machine; The Factory Set; Charlie's Dance; Charlie at the Assembly Line Belt; The Ballet; Visions; The Gamin; Charlie and the Warden; Alone and Hungry; Smile (Love Theme); In the City; Valse; The Sleeping Girl; Ten Days; At The Picture; Later That Night; The Toy Waltz; Closing Title
1940 *The Great Dictator*: Napoli March; Falling Star; Zigeuner; Ze Boulevardier; March Militaire
1942 *The Gold Rush*: On the Trail; Georgina at the Door; Dance of the Rolls; Country Dance
1947 *Monsieur Verdoux*: A Paris Boulevard; Tango Bitterness; Rumba
1952 *Limelight*: The Theme from Limelight (vocal version: Eternally); Ballet Introduction; Reunion; The Waltz; Terry's Theme; The Polka
1957 *A King in New York*: Mandolin Serenade; Now That It's Ended; The Spring Song; Weeping Willows; Bathtub Nonsense; Park Avenue Waltz; The Paperhangers
1959 *The Chaplin Revue*: The Chaplin Revue Theme
1959 *A Dog's Life*: Theme; Labour Exchange; Dog Chase; Green Lantern Rag; Coffee and Cakes; Flat Feet; The Shimmy; Song Triste; Robbers; Green Lantern Snag; Progression Rag; Dog Diggin'
1959 *Shoulder Arms*: Sauerkraut March; Shell Happy; Changing Guard; The Post; Over the Top; Blues; Peace; Tree Camouflage; Suspense; Mysterioso March; The Enemy; Agitato; D Minor Waltz; Inner March; Bringing Home the Bacon
1959 *The Pilgrim*: Bound for Texas; Jitters; Hope and Faith; The Deacon Presents
1967 *A Countess from Hong Kong*: My Star; This Is My Song; The Ambassador Retires; Crossing the Dance Floor; The Three Ladies; Perdu; The Deb Shakes; Chamber Music; Taxi Waltz; A Countess from Hong Kong; Change Partners; Bonjour Madame; Hudson Goes to Bed; The Ill-fitting Dress; The Countess Sleeps; Gypsy Caprice; Tango Natascha

1970 *The Circus*: The Circus

Recordings by Charles Chaplin
1925 *Sing a Song/With You Dear in Bombay* (Brunswick 2912)
Abe Lyman's California Orchestra conducted by Charlie Chaplin; Vocal: Charles Kaley
1957 *Mandolin Serenade/The Spring Song* (HMV POP 370)
Orchestra Conducted by Charles Chaplin

Recordings of Charles Chaplin's music
Modern Times (soundtrack) conducted by Alfred Newman
(UA S 5222)
Limelight (selection) Frank Chacksfield
(Decca F 10106)
A King in New York (selection) Norrie Paramor
(Columbia SEG 7720)
The Chaplin Revue (selection) Eric Spear
(Brunswick LAT 8345)
A Countess from Hong Kong (selection) Lambert Williamson
(Brunswick AXA 4544)
Chaplin Stan Butcher and his Warm Strings
(Fontana SFL 13207)
A Tribute to Charles Chaplin Stanley Black
(Decca PFS 4246)
Great Chaplin Film Themes Johnny Douglas Superstereo Sound
(RCA CDS 1114)
Music from the Films of Charlie Chaplin Michel Villard
(Pye NSPL 28173)

Chronological Bibliography

1915 *The Charlie Chaplin Scream Book* Draycott M. Dell
1915 *The Charlie Chaplin Fun Book* Albert T. Brown
1916 *Charlie Chaplin's Own Story* Charles Chaplin
1917 *The Chronicles of Charlie Chaplin* Langford Reed
1917 *Charlie Chaplin's Comic Capers* Elzie C. Segar
1917 *Charlie Chaplin in the Movies* Elzie C. Segar
1917 *Charlie Chaplin in the Air* Elzie C. Segar
1917 *Charlie Chaplin's Funny Stunts* Elzie C. Segar
1917 *The Charlie Chaplin Book*
1920 *Charlie Chaplin's Methods* (Cinema Course Lesson 2) Elsie Codd
1922 *My Trip Abroad* (GB: *My Wonderful Visit*) Charles Chaplin, Monta Bell
1922 *Charlie Chaplin* Louis Delluc
1923 *Chaplin* V. B. Shklousky
1924 *Charlie Chaplin* Gerhard Ausleger
1924 *Charlot* Disque Vert
1927 *Le Passion de Charlie Chaplin* Edouard Raymond
1927 *Charles Chaplin* Henry Poulaille
1927 *Charlie Chaplin* Robert Florey
1929 *Charlie Chaplin: Bericht Seines Lebens* Erich Burger
1930 *El Genio del Septimo Arte: Apologia de Charlot* Santiago Aguila
1931 *Charlie Chaplin: His Life and Art* William D. Bowman
1931 *Charlot* Philippe Soupault
1933 *La Verité sur Charlie Chaplin* Carlyle T. Robinson
1935 *Charlot, ou la Naissance d'un Mythe* Pierre Leprohon
1935 *Charlie Chaplin Intimé* May Reeves
1940 *Charlie Chaplin: King of Tragedy* Gerith Von Ulm
1945 *An Index to the Films of Charles Chaplin* Theodore Huff
1946 *Charlie Chaplin* Pierre Leprohon
1946 *Charles Spencer Chaplin* P. Ataseva, S. Achuskov
1948 *Chaplin, Last of the Clowns* Parker Tyler
1949 *La Figura e l'Arte di Charlie Chaplin* Bleiman, Kozintzevi, Youtkevitch, Eisenstein
1951 *The Little Fellow* Peter Cotes, Thelma Niklaus
1952 *Vie de Charlot* Georges Sadoul
1952 *Charlie Chaplin* Theodore Huff
1952 *Monsieur Chaplin* Maurice Bessy, Robert Florey
1952 *The Great God Pan* (GB: *The Great Charlie*) Robert Payne
1954 *Charlie Chaplin le Self-made Myth* Jose-Augusto Franca
1954 *Chaplin the Immortal Tramp* R. J. Minney
1955 *Chaplin e la Critica* Glauco Viazzi
1955 *Charlie Chaplin* Georges Sadoul

1957 *Charlot et la Fabulation Chaplinesque* Jean Mitry
1959 *Don Quixote e Carlito* Oliveira, Silva
1959 *Di Velt Fun Charlie Chaplin* David Matis
1959 *Charles Spencer Chaplin* G. A. Avenarius
1960 *My Father Charlie Chaplin* Charles Chaplin jr, N. Rau, M.Rau
1960 *Charlie Chaplin* Aleksandr V. Kukarkin
1963 *Charles Chaplin* Barthelmy Amengual
1964 *My Autobiography* Charles Chaplin
1965 *The Picture History of Charlie Chaplin* Gerald McDonald
1965 *The Films of Charlie Chaplin* Gerald McDonald, Michael Conway, Mark Ricci
1966 *Charles Chaplin* Marcel Martin
1966 *I Couldn't Smoke the Grass on My Father's Lawn* Michael Chaplin
1966 *My Life with Chaplin* Lita Grey Chaplin
1968 *Charlie Chaplin: Early Comedies* Isabel Quigley
1970 *Charles Chaplin* Pierre Leprohon
1971 *Chaplin i Sverige* Uno Asplund
1971 *Focus on Chaplin* Donald MacCaffrey
1972 *Il Tutto Chaplin* Francesco Savio
1972 *Charles Chaplin* Maurice Bessy, Robin Livio
1972 *Tout Chaplin* Jean Mitry
1972 *Charlie Chaplin und Seine Filme* Joe Hembus
1973 *Chaplin's Films* Uno Asplund

Notes to the Text

1 *My Autobiography* by Charles Chaplin
2 *Charlie Chaplin's Own Story* by Charles Chaplin
3 *Charlie the Immortal Tramp* by R. J. Minney
4 *Picture Play* April 1916
5 *Comedy Films* by John Montgomery
6 *City of Encounters* by Thomas Burke
7 *My Father Charlie Chaplin* by Charles Chaplin jr
8 *The Era* 11 May 1901
9 *Film Weekly* 4 April 1931
10 Mrs E. Turner Dauncey January 1951
11 *Photoplay* July 1915
12 *The Era* 11 July 1903
13 *The Era* 18 July 1903
14 *The Era* 1 August 1903
15 *The Stage* 1 May 1906
16 *The Era* 22, 29 September 1906; 29 June 1907
17 *The Little Fellow* by Cotes and Nicklaus
18 *The Era* 14 September 1907
19 *The Era* 18 June 1904
20 *The Era* 30 April 1910
21 *Variety* October 1910
22 *King of Comedy* by Cameron Shipp
23 *Moving Picture World* 7 February 1914
24 *Kinematograph Monthly Film Record* July 1914
25 *Classic Film Collector* Spring 1970
26 *Moving Picture World* 7 March 1914
27 *Moving Picture World* 21 March 1914
28 *Moving Picture World* 28 March 1914
29 *Moving Picture World* 15 August 1914
30 *Moving Picture World* 26 September 1914
31 *Moving Picture World* 24 October 1914
32 *Moving Picture World* 14 November 1914
33 *Moving Picture World* 26 December 1914
34 *Moving Picture World* 6 February 1915
35 *Photoplay* February 1915
36 *Photoplay* July 1915
37 *Moving Picture World* 13 February 1915
38 *Moving Picture World* 15 May 1915
39 *The Great God Pan* by Robert Payne
40 *Moving Picture World* 29 May 1915
41 *Pictures & Picturegoer* 22 April 1916
42 *Moving Picture World* 26 June 1915
43 *Moving Picture World* 6 May 1915
44 *Moving Picture World* 22 April 1915
45 *Moving Picture World* 3 June 1915
46 *Moving Picture World* 29 April 1915
47 *Moving Picture World* 11 March 1915
48 *Film Weekly* 28 February 1931
49 *American Magazine* November 1918
50 *Moving Picture World* 28 October 1916
51 *Moving Picture World* 30 December 1916
52 *Liberty* 29 July 1933
53 *Evening Journal* February 1931
54 BBC Interview 1952

Index

Page references in italics indicate illustrations